SUBSIDIA BIBLICA

30

subsidia biblica – 30

JOHANNES BEUTLER

Judaism and the Jews
in the Gospel of John

EDITRICE PONTIFICIO ISTITUTO BIBLICO – ROMA 2006

ISBN 88-7653-633-7

© E.P.I.B. – Roma – 2006

Iura editionis et versionis reservantur

EDITRICE PONTIFICIO ISTITUTO BIBLICO

Piazza della Pilotta, 35 - 00187 Roma, Italia

INTRODUCTION

In this book, I am publishing a course of lectures that was given during the first semester of the academic year 2004/20005 at the Pontifical Biblical Institute and at the Cardinal Bea Centre for Jewish Studies in the Pontifical Gregorian University in Rome. It was the insistence of the Revd James Swetnam SJ, the editor of this present series, who invited me to publish the course, that persuaded me to do this, contrary to my usual practice. I am grateful to him, therefore, for his encouragement. The links of the Fourth Gospel with its literary environment, an environment not only Hellenistic but also Jewish, aroused my interest at the time of my studies for the Licence at the Pontifical Biblical Institute and for the Doctorate in Theology at the Pontifical Gregorian University with Professors Ignace de la Potterie SJ and Donatien Mollat SJ. In the nineteen seventies, I began to take part in a group in Germany which was concerned with Jewish-Christian dialogue. Subsequently, I continued this activity in Italy, above all in the meetings at Camaldoli. Between 1996 and 2000, I collaborated on the document 'The Jewish People and their Sacred Scriptures in the Christian Bible' published by the Pontifical Biblical Commission in 2001. In March 2000, during the inauguration of the new Centre for the Study of Christianity at the Hebrew University of Jerusalem, I had the opportunity to read a paper on the subject of 'The Identity of the Jews for the Readers of John'. On such occasions as these I have been able to experience a new feeling of trust which is growing up between Jews and Christians after the tragedies of the last century. I am grateful to all those who have collaborated in the realisation of the project which is this book. Besides the Revd J. Swetnam, my particular thanks go Dr Michael Tait of Mirfield who recently completed his Licence at the Biblicum. To all of these and to the staff of the Pontifical Biblical Institute Press, I offer my warmest thanks.

Rome, December 1, 2006

N. B. The abbreviations for series, reviews and collective works are taken in this volume from S. SCHWERTNER, *Internationales Abkürzungsverzeichnis für Theologie und Grenzgebiete,* Berlin – New York: de Gruyter ²1992.

Lecture I

The Structure of John's Gospel and the Jewish Liturgy

Bibliography:

AILEEN GUILDING, *The Fourth Gospel and Jewish Worship*, Oxford: Clarendon 1960; D. MOLLAT, 'L'Évangile selon Saint Jean' in: ID., F.-M. BRAUN, *L'Évangile et les Lettres de Saint Jean* (La Sainte Bible de Jérusalem), Paris: du Cerf ²1960,7-193; R. E. BROWN, *The Gospel according to John,* I-II (AncB 29/29A), Garden City, NY: Doubleday 1966-1970; M. RISSI, 'Der Aufbau des Vierten Evangeliums' *NTS* 29 (1983) 48-54; J. STALEY, 'The Structure of John's Prologue: Its Implications for the Gospel's Narrative Structure', *CBQ* 48 (1986) 241-264; G. MLAKUZHYIL, *The Christocentric Literary Structure of the Fourth Gospel* (AnBib 117), Rome: Biblical Institute Press 1987; CH. H. GIBLIN, 'The Tripartite Narrative Structure of John's Gospel', *Bib.* 71 (1990) 449-468; H. THYEN, Johannes 10 im Kontext des Vierten Evangeliums, in: J. BEUTLER – R. T. FORTNA, ed., *The Shepherd Discourse of John 10 and its Context* (MSSNTS 67), Cambridge: University Press 1991, 116-134; F. F. SEGOVIA, 'The Journeys of the Word of God: A Reading of the Plot of the Fourth Gospel', in: R. A. CULPEPPER – ID., *The Fourth Gospel From a Literary Perspective* (Semeia 53), Atlanta, GA: Scholars Press 1991, 23-54; ID., 'The Journeys of Jesus to Jerusalem', in: A. DENAUX, ed., *John and the Synoptics* (BEThL 101), Leuven: University Press 1992, 535-541; J. BEUTLER, *Studien zu den johanneischen Schriften* (SBAB 25), Stuttgart: Katholisches Bibelwerk 1998; F. J. MOLONEY, *The Gospel of John* (Sacra Pagina 13), Collegeville, Minnesota: Liturgical Press. A Michael Glazier Book 1998.

The connection between John's Gospel and Judaism is not limited to any particular thematic or historical link. In fact a reflection of the Jewish liturgy can be found in the very structure of the Fourth Gospel. It seems as if the whole narrative section of the Gospel is determined by the Jewish liturgical year with its three pilgrimage feasts to Jerusalem: Passover, Pentecost and Tabernacles. Before explaining this point of view, it is appropriate to list briefly the most recent proposals concerning the structure of John's Gospel.

1. *Authors who deny a discernible structure*

It is a common view, even among more recent scholars, to deny that there is a discernible structure in the Fourth Gospel. This is the predominant view in Germany (cf, for example, W. G. Kümmel, R. Schnackenburg). The reason for this position is probably to be found in the historical orientation of the classic German contributions to the subject and in the widely adopted theories of sources, literary strata or internal displacements in the text of John. Thus the diachronic paradigm prevails over the synchronic one.

2. *Various proposals for structuring the Fourth Gospel*

A) Thematic Proposals

The most accepted division of the Fourth Gospel is that in two parts, normally with the pivot in Jn 13:1, the beginning of the Last Supper of Jesus with his own as preparation for the Passion. Thus, in his commentary (1941), despite the various displacements of the pericopes which he detects, Bultmann sees a division of the text of the Fourth Gospel into two parts: Jn 2-12, 'The revelation of the *doxa* before the world'. And 13-20, 'the revelation of the *doxa* before the community'. Chapter 1 would constitute the prologue and the introduction; Chapter 21 the epilogue and a supplement. Similarly, C. H. Dodd[1] separates Jn 2-12, 'The Book of Signs' from 13-20, 'The Book of the Passion'. Various sections of the first part are structured round the different words of Jesus ('Εγώ εἰμι and other key concepts). R. E. Brown modifies Dodd's proposal, changing the title 'The Book of the Passion' (Chapters 13-20) to 'The Book of Glory', something which appears to be a more felicitous choice. The first part of the Gospel is divided by Brown into two sections: 'From Cana to Cana' (Chapters 2-4) and 'Jesus and the Principal Feasts of the Jews' (Chapters 5-10), with Chapters 11-12 interpreted as a transitional passage to the account of the Passion and Resurrection of Jesus. Here the thematic division has already been replaced by a more specific

---

[1] *The Interpretation of the Fourth Gospel,* Cambridge 1953.

structure which also includes spatial, chronological and liturgical elements.

B) Dramatic Proposals

For some authors, like J. L. Martyn,[2] the 'drama' of the conflict between Jesus and the Jews lies at the centre of interest and, at the same time, is functional in the structuring of John's Gospel. However, this conflict develops throughout the whole Gospel so that its steps are not easily distinguishable as specific elements in the structuring of the Gospel. A similar approach has been adopted by Mark Stibbe in his various publications and by Ludger Schenke in his commentary: Johannes (Düsseldorf: Patmos, 1998). The latter arrives at a division of the Fourth Gospel into two main sections: after the Prologue, the 'descent' of Jesus and his manifestation in the world (1:19-12:36) with a first Epilogue in 12:37-50; and then the 'ascent' and the manifestation of Jesus before the disciples in 13:1-20:29 with a second Epilogue in 20:30f before a double ending in 21:1-24:25. Thus, after the two main sections, there is an evaluation of the mission and revelation of Jesus, first negative, then positive (12:37-50; 20:30f).

C) Typological approaches

According to some authors, John's Gospel, or at least a part of it (such as the Prologue or the first week of Jesus' activity) can be explained by means of references to Genesis or Exodus taken up as structural models: thus, in the coming of Jesus the work of creation or redemption is re-enacted. But although these are aspects of great importance, their usefulness as structural indicators in the Fourth Gospel appears to be limited.

D) Symbolic Approaches

Every so often attempts are made to determine the structure of the Fourth Gospel with a reference to numerical symbolism. Wholes with three, five or seven parts (cf the seven 'I am' sayings or the seven 'Signs' of Jesus) have been detected. There are also suggestions based

---

[2] *History and Theology in the Fourth Gospel*, New York: Harper & Row 1968.

on word statistics. In general, Johannine research is hesitant about attempts of this kind. They do, in fact, highlight the difference between the Gospel of John and the Book of the Apocalypse where the numerical symbolism is undisputed. The number 'seven' recurs fifty times in the Apocalypse and never in John's Gospel. Immediately this leads us away from attributing a facile numerical symbolism to the Fourth Gospel.

E) Approaches based on chronology or liturgy

It seems that the Jewish feasts have an important role to play in the structure of the Fourth Gospel, and for this reason, in the French original of the Jerusalem Bible, D. Mollat divided it according to the Jewish liturgical calendar. After the 'Opening Week' (1:19-2:12), there follow the First Feast of the Passover in Jerusalem (2:13); the Second (unnamed) in 5:1 (probably *Shavuot* = Pentecost); then the Passover in 6:4; The Feast of Tabernacles in 7:2; *Chanukka* (The Dedication of the Temple) in 10:22; and finally, The Last Passover in 11:55, 12:1, 13:1 until 19:42. This proposal is worth mentioning for the combination of elements of content, place and time which are found in it. We shall return to this later (cf Lecture III).

F) Approaches based on topology

Finally, topological matters have again been considered important for the structuring of the Fourth Gospel. M. Rissi (cf supra) discovers three journeys of Jesus before his last journey to Jerusalem. This begins in non-Jewish or pagan territory, then passes through Galilee and leads finally to Jerusalem: 1:19-3:36; 4:1-5:47; 6:1-10:39. At this point the last departure for Jerusalem begins (10:40-12:41), the farewell of Jesus to his own (13:1- 14:31) - Chapters 15-17 are held to be an addition - and the return of the Son to the Father (18:1-20:31) - Chapter 21 is a further addition. At the beginning of everything stands the Prologue. This results in a structure of seven sections, with the repetition – twice – of three sections, after the Prologue, and with the turning point at 10:40. J. Staley agrees with Rissi, above all with the last suggestion (as also H. Thyen of Heidelberg in his contribution on Jn 10) with the sole modification that the climax is to be found in Jn 11:1 (so also Thyen). Staley sees the idea of the 'journey' already prepared for in the

Prologue where the descent and ascent of the Logos is described. Thus we have the outline of four journeys: 1:19-3:36; 4:1-6:71; 7:1-10:42 and 11:1-21:25. The route of the first part of the Gospel (1:19-10:42) leads Jesus from Bethany beyond the Jordan to Bethany near Jerusalem (1:28; 11:1, 18). The central figure who accompanies the movement is John the Baptist, mentioned for the first time in the narrative at 1:28 and at the end in 10:42. He is 'replaced' by Lazarus, the 'one loved' by Jesus (11:5), and by the 'Beloved Disciple', the two being the same person according to some authors (H. Thyen, W. Schenk). The investigations into the structure and vocabulary of the various sections lean on Staley's proposal concerning the general structure of John. However, despite its various positive points, Staley's proposal is not completely convincing. Problems remain with the second journey with its ending in Galilee (Jn 6) and the fourth which is difficult to integrate in the journey-scheme (even more so when Chapter 21 is included – Rissi is more convincing here). In his two contributions, F. F. Segovia sees more clearly that the journeys of Jesus regularly lead to Jerusalem. Like Rissi, he acknowledges three journeys (1:19-3:36; 4:1-5:42; 6:1-10, 42) before the last and decisive one from 11:1. Such journeys are the means by which the reader is enabled to share in the destiny of the hero, but he seems to undervalue the importance of the principal Jewish feasts, correlated as they are with the journeys of Jesus, and the internal structure of John.

G) Combined Approaches

In recent years one can detect an increasing emphasis on combining the various formal and conceptual criteria which come into play in the elaboration of the structure of John. This emphasis is discernible, for example, in the great work of the Indian scholar, G. Mlakuzhyil, a disciple of I. de la Potterie of the Pontifical Biblical Institute. For Mlakuzhyil, it is Christology that determines the structure of John. After a Christocentric introduction (1:1-2:11), Mlakuzhyil identifies 'The Book of the Signs of Jesus' (2:1-12:50), with the account of the Wedding at Cana as a transitional section (2:1-11), and 'the Book of the Hour of Jesus' (11:1-20:29), with 11:1-12:50 as a transitional section (cf above for H. Thyen). There follow the 'Christocentric conclusion' in 20.30f and an Epilogue in 21:1-25. The placing of 2:1-11 and 11:1-12:50 agrees with both the preceding and following contexts. The confining of the Jewish liturgical year to the section of the great controversies of Jesus with 'the Jews' of Jerusalem in 5:1-10:42 appears less convincing.

The structural proposal made by C. H. Giblin is also characterised by the combination of formal and conceptual criteria. Giblin starts from the spatial and temporal indications and from the dramatic elements. In 1:19-4:54, the universal mission of Jesus is described; in 5:1-10:42 it is the turn of the hostility against him in the great controversies; from 11:1, his love for his own to the end. It remains the case that the true transition to the second part is reached only at 13:1 so that the classical division into two parts retains its force. Once again, the question remains whether the spatial and chronological elements of the text have met with sufficient attention in the elaboration of the narrative structure of John.

3. *Synthesis*

We too, in the same way, seek to combine the methods employed up to now. Thus we shall respect the topographical, chronological, liturgical, formal and material elements of our Gospel. From D. Mollat (cf *supra*) we shall take up the important role of the Jewish feasts; from Rissi, Staley and Segovia the importance of the journeys of Jesus leading up to his final ascent towards Jerusalem. It is appropriate, however, to regard the journeys of Jesus as journeys of pilgrimage to Jerusalem on the occasions of the principal feasts of the Jews. It is possible that some additions have been supplied to the original text. An annual cycle of Jewish feasts of pilgrimage formed the original framework of the narrative part of John between 2:13 and 11:55. Jesus sets out on the way to Jerusalem four times: for the first Passover in 2:13, for the anonymous feast (probably Pentecost) in 5:1; for the Feast of Tabernacles in 7:2, and for the last Passover in 11:1 (mentioned afterwards in 11:55, 12:1, 13:1). For the Passover of 6:4, there is no reference to Jerusalem. The whole of Chapter 6 could well have been added under the influence of the Synoptic parallels.[3] The Feast of the

---

[3] cf. J. BEUTLER, 'Zur Struktur von Joh 6,' SNTU Serie A 16, Linz 1991, 89-104: 89 with note 2; now in: ID., *Studien*, 247-262: 247 with 2.

Dedication of the Temple, in 10:22, can be incorporated into this scheme without the necessity for a new journey to Jerusalem because Jesus is already there. From the theological point of view, Jesus brings to fulfilment both the sacred times and the sacred spaces of Israel. (The Temple is placed at the beginning and at the end!) Exegetes rightly see an 'Opening Week' in the activity of Jesus in 1:19-2:12 with its scheme of seven days at the beginning of the Gospel, and at the end, the week when Jesus returns to the Father, a week that begins with the anointing of Jesus 'six days before the Passover' in 12:1. Cf also the six days of the story of Lazarus in Jn 11!

Aileen Guilding (op. cit.) has sought to detect the Jewish lectionary behind the structure of John. Her various attempts at reconstruction, however, have not met with acceptance by her colleagues. Perhaps it is more important to limit oneself to the content of the feasts according to the Biblical or Proto-Rabbinic tradition. The Feast of the Passover is, of course, the feast of the liberation of Israel which, as such, fits in well with the structure of John: Jesus begins and ends his activity on such a feast. Already from antiquity, there has been much discussion as to the nature of the feast in Jn 5:1. Already St John Chrysostom (*In Joannem homiliae* 59.203.24f) thinks of the Feast of Pentecost (which follows the Passover feast, mentioned in Jn 2:13, as a feast of pilgrimage); Epiphanius of Salamis (Haer. 2.282.32f) thinks of either Pentecost or Tabernacles. In the Mishnah (Meg. 3,5) Deut 16:9-12, the law with regard to the celebration of Pentecost as a feast of pilgrimage to Jerusalem, is prescribed as a reading for this feast. Similarly in the Mishnah (Rosh ha-shanah 1,2), Pentecost is named as one of the feasts on which the (divine) judgement takes place – cf Jn 5:19-30. In the later Rabbinic tradition, Pentecost becomes the feast which commemorates the gift of the Law and its renewal.[4] The most ancient texts are from the third century of our era, but the tradition could well be earlier. This would fit in well with the theme of faithfulness to Moses and his writings in Jn 5:31-47. For the Feast of Tabernacles, mentioned in Jn 7:2, recent commentators mention the rites of this feast (described in

---

[4] Cf. Encyplopaedia Judaica 14, Jerusalem: Keter [*sine anno*], 1319-1322.

the Mishnah, Sukka, chs 4-5): a procession to the Pool of Siloam to draw the waters from that spring, and a festive illumination of the Temple during this feast. Cf Jn 7:37ff and 8:12; 9:5.

Lecture II
The Sabbath

Bibliography:

H.L. STRACK – P. BILLERBECK, *Kommentar zum Neuen Testament aus Talmud und Midrasch*, II, Munich: Beck ²1956; H. WEISS, 'The Sabbath in the Fourth Gospel', *JBL* 110 (1991) 311-321; J.-M. SEVRIN, 'Jésus et le sabbat dans le quatrième évangile', in: *La loi dans l'un et l'autre testament*, ed. C. Focant (LD 168), Paris: du Cerf 1997, 226-242; T. THATCHER, 'The Sabbath Trick: Unstable Irony in the Fourth Gospel', *JSNT* 76 (1999) 53-77; M. ASIEDU-PEPRAH, *Johannine Sabbath Conflicts as Juridical Controversy* (WUNT II 132), Tübingen: Mohr Siebeck 2001.

As we have seen, the Jewish liturgical year has an important role to play in John's Gospel. The same can be said of the Sabbath. The word σάββατον is encountered thirteen times in the Fourth Gospel (Jn 5:9, 10, 16, 18; 7:22, 23, twice; 9:14, 16; 19:31, twice; 20:1, 19). The more important texts are the controversies on the Sabbath in Jn 5:1-18; 7:19-24; 9:14-16.

1. *The historical Approach*

John is seen to be nearest to the Synoptic tradition in the Passion Narrative despite some problems with the chronology. According to all four gospels, Jesus dies on the day of the 'preparation', probably preparation for the Sabbath (παρασκευή, cf. Mt 27:62; Mk 15:42; Lk 23:54; Jn 19:14, 31, 42). In Mark, this day of the 'preparation' is called προσάββατον, 'the day before the Sabbath'; John, on the other hand, speaks of a 'preparation for the Passover' (19:42), that is 'the day of the preparation in the week of the Passover (cf W. Bauer, Dict., *ad vocem*). The women come on 'the first day of the week' to visit the tomb of Jesus (cf Mt 28:1; Mk 16:1; Lk 24:1: Jn 20:1). In all four gospels, the disciples of Jesus, men and women, appear to respect the Sabbath. The men take Jesus' body from the cross before the beginning of the Sabbath (Jn 19:31 parr), and the women go to the sepulchre only after the Sabbath (Jn 20:1 parr).

Of the three passages which tell of a dispute between Jesus and the Jewish authorities following a miracle done on the Sabbath, the healing of the paralytic (Jn 5:1-18 with the subsequent debate in Jn 7:22f) is the nearest to the Synoptic tradition. In Mk 2:1-3:6, there is a section often labelled 'Galilean Controversies'. At the beginning stands the cure of a paralytic with verbal links with Jn 5:1-13 and a dispute over the authority of Jesus to forgive sins; this is followed by controversies between Jesus and the Pharisees over fasting and on the right of Jesus and his disciples to pluck ears of grain on the Sabbath; and at the end we find the account of the cure of the man with the paralysed hand by Jesus in a synagogue on the Sabbath day. With this last passage, Jn 5:1-18; 7:22f shares the Sabbath controversy. Both in Mark's tradition and in John, the validity of the Sabbath law does not come into question. In Mark, two perspectives are offered: a humanitarian principle, according to which 'the Sabbath is made for man and not man for the Sabbath' (Mk 2:27), and a Christological principle: 'So the Son of Man is Lord even of the Sabbath' (Mk 2:28). We see that John is located in this double tradition. In the debate of Jn 7:22ff, he puts himself in the position of the sick man who is perfectly entitled to, nay must find salvation and health on the Sabbath day. In Chapters 5 and 9, on the other hand, the Christological principle is dominant but again without the validity of the Sabbath law being put into question. Whether or not the Sabbath law is still valid is not discussed but only whether or in what way it finds its fulfilment in the work of Jesus carried out on the basis of his oneness with the Father.

2. *The literary Approach*

Some recent authors have made a special study of the literary aspect of the Sabbath controversies in Jn 5 and 7 on the one hand and Jn 9 on the other.

Tom Thatcher starts out from observing that the fact that the miracles of Jesus which are recounted in Jn 5 and 9 take place on the Sabbath is introduced only after the narration of the miracle: Jn 5:9 and 9:14. According to Thatcher, the readers are not expecting this. One could even say that the readers are taken for a ride by the narrator! The passage takes an unexpeceted twist and so could even be called a 'Sabbath Trick'. In so far as the passage does not conform to the expected, one could speak here of 'irony'. In speaking of irony, Thatcher distinguishes two types: 'stable' and 'unstable' (cf p 54). In 'stable' irony, only the characters in the story are 'deceived' but no the reader. In 'unstable' irony, however, the reader too is 'deceived'. He is informed about an important aspect of the story only after the account itself, and has to begin again to understand the story. Thatcher finds this second type of irony in the two accounts of healings carried out by Jesus on the Sabbath in Jn 5 and 9. What is the point of this literary technique? According to Thatcher, John employs this technique to arouse the reader's interest and to open up new horizons for him: he must free himself from preconceived ideas and open himself up to a new way of understanding Jesus and his activity. For Thatcher this opens the way for a 'deconstruction' which allows one's own understanding of the text to become free for a further re-reading.

Thatcher's contribution is undoubtedly original. It is to be doubted, however, if it is equally useful. To suppose that the author of a gospel centred so much on the concept of 'the truth' would deliberately take his readers for a ride seems hard to imagine! The distinction between various literary strata in the two accounts mentioned could be the simplest solution to the problem. In both cases, a primitive account which is not connected with the problem of Sabbath observance has been joined, secondarily, to the problem of Sabbath observance on the part of Jesus. According to many authors, it would be the evangelist himself (and not a pre-Johannine or post-Johannine redactor) who has introduced this dimension in order to develop his Christology and soteriology.

The contribution of Martin Asiedu-Peprah (from Ghana) deserves more attention. He studied for his Licence at the Biblicum from 1993 to 1997 and subsequently elaborated his thesis for the Catholic University of Australia. Drawing his inspiration from the Revd Pietro Bovati, the author studies the *rîb-pattern* in the prophetic texts of the Old Testament and applies it to the Johannine controversies on the Sabbath. The difference between the *rîb* and the trial consists of the fact that in the *rîb*, two parties dispute over a judicial question without a third party whereas in a trial, this third party hears the case, judges and decides. According to Asiedu-Peprah,, the debates between Jesus and 'the Jews' on the Sabbath in Jn 5 and 9 are of the *rîb* type without the presence of a third party who judges; they are not of the 'trial' type as has been generally maintained. This contribution is certainly valid. However, in this connection, one could pose some questions and make some observations. It is true that the controversies of Jn 5-10 have a juridical aspect, but it is equally undeniable that they are, above all, a literary technique with which the fourth evangelist expounds his message, both Christological and soteriological. In this way, the speeches of Jesus in these chapters are at one and the same time 'self-defence in a lawsuit' and 'revelatory discourses' (*Offenbarungsreden* as Rudolf Bultmann called them). The juridical aspect helps to develop the message and the theology of the fourth evangelist. In Johannine research, the prevailing opinion is that the aim of the Fourth Gospel is not that of convincing non-believers about the claims of Jesus to be, himself, the Messiah and the Son of God, but rather to strengthen the faith of readers who already believe (cf the present subjunctive πιστεύητε in Jn 20:31, which is today considered to be the preferred reading).

Another observation can be added. It is true that in the controversies between Jesus and 'the Jews' of Jerusalem over the Sabbath in Jn 5, 7 and 9, there is no explicit reference to a third judicial authority; but it is equally true that such an authority is never far away. From Chapter 7 on, the intention of Jesus' opponents to get rid of him becomes ever more clearly evident: 'After this, Jesus went about in Galilee; he would not go about in Judaea because the Jews sought to kill him' (7:1). In this context, it is clear that in the thought of the Fourth Evangelist, 'the Jews' are acting as one with the contemporary leaders of the Jewish people: 'the chief priests and Pharisees' (7:45), are probably a specific definition of the Sanhedrin. These have at their beck and call 'officers' (ibid) who are empowered to arrest Jesus. At the end of Chapter 8 (8:59), the opponents of Jesus take up stones to throw at him, the same action is repeated in Chapter 10 (10:31), and, finally, the group of opponents tries to arrest Jesus (10:39). Jesus saves himself for a brief period before being arrested definitively (18:12), condemned and put to death (19:16). Thus, the controversies between Jesus and 'the Jews' are not debates between equals with a result that is open to the strength of the arguments. It is the political power that prevails. For this reason, the questions put to Jesus by 'the Jews' have an aspect of a trial about them. In any case, it remains true that in the perspective of the fourth evangelist the true 'trial' is unfolding between Jesus, the judge, and 'the world', which does not want to believe. This aspect of 'krisis' was developed many years ago by Josef Blank,[5] and subsequently by various authors including the present one.[6]

3. The theological and inter-religious approach

Jn 5. As Sevrin has emphasised, the two accounts of the healings performed by Jesus, in Jn 5 and 9, have many characteristics in common: the role of a pool in Jerusalem: the fact that the Sabbath is mentioned as the day of the healing only after the account itself; a dialogue between the person who has been cured and 'the Jews'; and a final encounter of that person with Jesus. Another common element is the fact that the cured person did not know who Jesus was before. In Chapter 5, the dialogue between 'the Jews' and the cured man concerns the (Rabbinic) prohibition of carrying anything at all from one place to another on the Sabbath. Jesus, however, had commanded the sick man to take up his bed and walk (Jn 5:8; cf Mt 9:6; Mk 2:11; Lk 5:24). 'The Jews' subsequently want to know who had healed the paralytic. He does not know who it was, but Jesus meets him afterwards in the Temple and tells him not to sin any more lest something worse befall him. After that, he goes to 'the Jews' to tell them that it was Jesus who had cured him. In contrast with the man born blind who was cured, this fellow does not seem to have come to believe in Jesus; on the contrary, his informing the Jewish authorities has something of the whiff of a denunciation.

The standpoint of 'the Jews', according to which it is not permissible to carry an object from one place to another on the Sabbath is confirmed by the Mishnah. The whole of the treatise 'Shabbat' is full of regulations as to what can or cannot be carried on a Sabbath day. The regulations are confirmed and stated clearly in the Tosefta and the two Talmuds. Cf the commentary by Strack-Billerbeck, II, 454-461. Of particular interest is a passage of the Mishnah (Shabb. 10,5, quoted in

---

[5] *Krisis*, Freiburg: Herder 1964.
[6] *Martyria*, FTS 10, Frankfurt a. M.: Knecht 1972.

part also by Str.-Bill., 461) according to which it is lawful to carry an invalid on a stretcher on the Sabbath but not to carry a dead man because the aim of the exemption from the law is the service performed for the sick man. According to this interpretation, the command given by Jesus remains unlawful within the perspective of the Rabbinic tradition. The justification for Jesus' command given to the paralytic is found in Jn 5 not in humanitarian considerations but in the context of theological reasoning. According to the beliefs of first century Judaism, God continues to work for the benefit of the creation even on the Sabbath: Jesus, therefore, being the Son of God, shares in this divine activity. The two activities which are reserved to God alone (and which he performs every day) are, according to Jn 5:21f, giving life and judging. Jewish parallels for this double activity of God even on the Sabbath are listed by Strack-Billerbeck II, 461f. From Hellenistic Judaism one could quote Philo of Alexandria, *Leg. All.* 1.3; from Rabbinical sources, relevant above all are the commentaries on Genesis *à propos* of Gen 2:2 such as Genesis Rabba 10,8; 11,8: in the first passage, the continuation of the work of creation by God even beyond the sixth day is asserted; in the second, the divine activity of rewarding the just and the wicked even on the Sabbath is also asserted. A fine passage taken from Exodus Rabba 30 describes the whole world as the house of God and full of the divine presence so much so that God can remain constantly active since he is within his own house! The Johannine Jesus leans in the direction of these reasonings. The single original aspect is that in Jn 5:19-30 he declares himself as one with the Father in his activity. The occasion of this messianic activity of Jesus is eschatological as is clearly expressed by the formula ἕως ἄρτι in Jn 5:17.

Jn 7. In Chapter 7, the controversy over the healing of the paralytic, described in Chapter 5, is resumed. If Chapter 6 has been added subsequently, the two passages follow each other without any problems. In vv 1-13 the decision of Jesus, afterwards modified (he goes 'in private'), not to go to the Feast of Tabernacles is described. In vv 14-24, there is a new confrontation with the Jews present in the Temple area over his observance of the Law and the healing performed on the Sabbath. In this case, Jesus argues on the basis of a principle recognised in the Judaism of the period (it belongs to the fourteen *middot* listed by Hillel) – the concept of 'from the light to the heavy' (*qal waḥomer*). The argument is as follows: if the Law allows the practice of circumcision on the Sabbath, thus allowing the amputation of part of a member, how much more lawful will be the healing of the whole human body. For this kind of reasoning there are parallels listed in Strack-Billerbeck II, 488. The Rabbis allow the healing of a person in danger of death even on the Sabbath (cf Tos. Shabb. 15,16; Talmud Babli Joma 85b: Rabbi El'azar ben Azarja , ca AD 100). The only difference is that Jesus heals a person who is not in danger of death. Given that in Chapter 7 of John the argumentation remains very close to the Jewish discussions, Weiss, following Bultmann, ascribes this passage to a source that precedes the discourses of Chapter 5. However that may be, the text, once taken up, becomes a Johannine text.

Jn 9. In Chapter 9 of John, the discussions about the healing performed by Jesus on the Sabbath dominate the second half of the chapter (vv 15-34). In this case, the fault committed by Jesus is not a command given to the person who has been healed, but an action which he himself has carried out; he mixes some clay and the spittle and anoints the eyes of the man born blind on the Sabbath. One such case is discussed explicitly in the Babylonian Talmud (Aboda Zara 28b with reference to a Rabbi of the third century: cf Strack-Billerbeck II 533f). Again, the Rabbis allow the healing of a damaged eye in an acute case, but not where the damage is chronic as with the man born blind. In this case, in Jn 9, the discussion shifts, once again, from the question whether Jesus can perform such a 'work' on the Sabbath to the question concerning his identity. Various answers are given. For 'the Jews', Jesus is not from God; he is a sinner (9:16, 24f), for the man born blind, Jesus is a prophet (9:17), and is 'a worshipper of God and does his will' (9:31), 'he is from God' (9:33). Thus Jesus is able to lead him to the confession of faith, expressed on bended knee (9:38), that he is 'the Son of man' (9:35-37). In the end, it turns out that the man who was blind sees not only with his physical eyes but also with the eyes of faith, and those who believe that they can see appear to be blind because they have not known or recognised Jesus. It is neither the man born blind nor his parents who are sinners (cf 9:2f) but those who

refuse to believe in Jesus (9:40f). Once again, John's Gospel goes way
beyond the halakhic discussions concerning the Sabbath Law and puts
the readers in the position of having to take sides for or against Jesus,
the one sent by the Father.

Lecture III

The Temple and the Synagogue

Bibliography:

J. FRÜHWALD-KÖNIG, *Tempel und Kult. Ein Beitrag zur Christologie des Johannesevangeliums* (BU 27), Regensburg: Pustet 1998; MARY M. COLOE, 'Raising the Johannine temple (John 19:19-37),' *ABR* 48 (2000) 47-58; W. RADL, "'Brecht diesen Tempel ab…" (Joh 2,19). Zum traditions- und religionsgeschichtlichen Umfeld johanneischen "Missverständnisses"', in: S. SCHREIBER – A. STIMPFLE, ed., *Johannes aenigmaticus. Studien zum Johannesevangelium für Herbert Leroy* (BU 29), Regensburg: Pustet 2001, 71-86; MARY M. COLOE, *God dwells with us. Temple symbolism in the fourth gospel*, Collegeville, Minn.: Liturgical Press 2001; R. LÓPEZ ROSAS, *La Señal del Templo. Jn 2,13-22. Redefinición Cristológica de lo Sacro*, México: Departamento de Publicaciones. Universidad Pontificia de México, A.C., 2001; U. BUSSE, *Das Johannesevangelium. Bildlichkeit, Diskurs und Ritual. Mit einer Bibliographie über den Zeitraum* 1986-1998 (BEThL 162), Leuven: University Press 2002; J. H. ULRICHSEN, 'Jesus – der neue Tempel? Ein kritischer Blick auf die Auslegung von Joh 2,13-22', in: D. E. AUNE – T. SELAND – J. H. ULRICHSEN, ed., *Neotestamentica et Philonica. Studies in honor of Peder Borgen* (NT.S 106), Leiden: Brill 2003, 202-214; C. UMOH, 'The temple in the fourth gospel,' in: M. LABAHN – K. SCHOLTISSEK – A. STROTMANN, ed., *Israel und seine Heilstraditionen im Johannesevangelium. Festgabe für Johannes Beutler SJ zum 70. Geburtstag*, Paderborn etc.: Schöningh 2004, 314-333; P. BORGEN, '"All my teaching was done in Synagogues…" (John 18,20)', in: G. VAN BELLE – J. G. VAN DER WATT – P. MARITZ, ed., *Theology and Christology in the Fourth Gospel* (BEThL 184), Leuven: University Press 2005, 223-224.

The Temple and the Synagogue belong to the central institutions of Judaism which have their place in the Fourth Gospel. The term ἱερόν recurs thirteen times in the Fourth Gospel. (Cf also ναός in Jn 2:19, 20, 21). This compares with eleven occurrences in Matthew, nine in Mark, fourteen in Luke; Acts knows twenty five instances of it, Paul only one (1 Cor 9:13 where he speaks of pagan sanctuaries). From these observations, the importance of the theme of the Temple for John is immediately apparent. His usage is exceeded only by Luke (Gospel and Acts = 39 occurences). We shall see that there is a fundamental difference between the two authors: for Luke, the story of Jesus begins and ends in Jerusalem; the account of Jesus' infancy begins in the Temple and it is in the Temple in Jerusalem that the story of the Church begins (Acts 1-2). It will be seen that this viewpoint is not shared by John.

The term συναγωγή recurs only twice in John (6:59; 18:20). The idea of being ἀποσυνάγωγος (Jn 9:22; 12:42: 16:2) is linked with it. The word συναγωγή is found fifty six times in the New Testament, above all in the Synoptic Gospels. In Paul, there is no example, in James, only one (James 2:2), in the Apocalypse two (2:9: 3:9). Thus a contrast is apparent both with Paul and with the Synoptic Gospels, but it is different in each case.

1. *The Temple as the place of Jesus' teaching in John*

The Temple appears in John's Gospel as the privileged place of Jesus' teaching activity. In his interrogation before Annas, the High Priest (cf Jn 18:20), Jesus says in Jn 18:20: 'I have spoken openly to the world; I have always taught in synagogues and in the temple, where all Jews come together; I have said nothing secretly' These words are based on the words of Jesus in the Synoptic tradition on the occasion of his arrest (Mk 14:49; Mt 26:55; Lk 22:53). The teaching of Jesus 'in the synagogue' has been added but finds little support in the Fourth Gospel itself apart from the teaching of Jesus in the synagogue at Capernaum (Jn 6:59). On this latter, see below, paragraph 3. According to Jn 5:14, Jesus finds the paralytic, whom he has healed, in the Temple and tells him to sin no more. The following occurrences of the word refer to Jesus' sojourn in the area of the Temple on the occasion of the Feast of Tabernacles and of the Dedication. Despite his initial hesitation, Jesus goes up to the Feast of Tabernacles and teaches in the Temple (7:14), even with a loud voice (7:28). There too occurs the encounter with the woman taken in adultery, according to one part of the manuscript tradition (8:2).

The teachings of Jesus reported in Jn 8 similarly take place in the Temple. After a clash with the Jewish authorities, Jesus withdraws from the Temple which increasingly becomes the place of opposition to him (8:59). One last time, the Temple is named in this connection in Jn 10:23: Jesus is in Jerusalem during the Feast of the Dedication and is teaching in the Temple. At the end of a final clash with 'the Jews', Jesus withdraws and escapes from their hands (10:39). From that moment, he never returns to the Temple. The pilgrims ask if he will come to the Feast of the Passover, but Jesus enters the Temple no more (11:56).

Also for Matthew and Mark, Jesus leaves the Temple after its 'cleansing' and the final controversies with the Jewish authorities (Mk 11-12; Mt 21-23). He delivers his last discourse (concerning the future of Jerusalem, the Temple its precincts (Mk 13; Mt 24) on the Mount of Olives, opposite the Temple (Mk 13:1; Mt 24:1). On this point the first two evangelists agree in contrast with Luke who does not describe the surroundings of Jesus' last discourse (cf Lk 24:5).

2. *The body of Jesus – the new Temple*

The cleansing of the Temple is recounted in John's Gospel right at the beginning of Jesus' public ministry (Jn 2:13-22). The theories concerning the change in the textual location of this scene are numerous: it seems to us that the fourth evangelist wanted to give a dramatic note to his whole account from the very start. On the other hand, the account of the cleansing of the Temple occurs now in John beside that of the Marriage at Cana in Jn 2:1-11. In the story of the Marriage at Cana, temporal categories predominate (before/after, lack/abundance, poor wine/good wine); in the account of the Cleansing of the Temple, on the other hand it is spatial categories that are dominant (Temple/expelling/from here/house of my Father). For this reason, it can be said that from day one, John presents Jesus as the one who sanctifies both the sacred times and sacred places of Israel.

In the Synoptic Gospels, the Account of the Cleansing of the Temple by Jesus has a messianic-eschatological character. Jesus enters the Sanctuary of Israel purifying it from its imperfections. He is hailed with messianic songs and hymns. However, no connection is established between Jesus himself and the Sanctuary. This happens only in John's Gospel. The fourth evangelist recounts words of Jesus attested in the Synoptic tradition but as words attributed to Jesus by the false witnesses in Mk 14:56 (par.): 'I will destroy this Temple that is made with hands, and in three days I will build another, not made with hands'. In John, Jesus himself uses these words but in the form of a warning directed to the Jews: 'Destroy this Temple, and in three days I will raise it up.' (2:19). In the perspective of the fourth evangelist, these words refer to the body of Jesus, only, for the moment, no one is able to understand this meaning. Jesus' enemies understand his words on the architectural level: if the Temple took forty six years to build, how could Jesus make a new sanctuary in only three days? The evangelist comments: 'But he spoke of the temple of his body. When therefore he was raised from the dead, his disciples remembered that he had said this; and they believed the scripture and the word which Jesus had spoken' (2:21f).

Various aspects of this passage deserve our attention. First: the identification of the body of Jesus with the Sanctuary of the Temple in Jerusalem. This is the most radical reinterpretation of theme of the Sanctuary of Israel in the Gospels. Commentators mention Paul who, in Rom 3:25, identifies Jesus with the 'kapporet', the covering of the Ark of the Covenant, the place of atonement according to the Old Covenant. We have noted the absence of the term ἱερόν in Paul.

A second aspect for the understanding of these words is the reference to the time of the Resurrection of Jesus in his own body. Recent authors (above all, the 'Swiss School': J. Zumstein, A. Dettwiler) highlight the importance of the time of the 'glorification' of Jesus for the understanding of his message. It is only from the post-Easter perspective that the message of Jesus can be understood.

The third aspect that deserves our attention is the connection between the Resurrection and the image of the body of Jesus understood as the divine Sanctuary. Some authors (such as R. López Rosas) identify the body of Jesus with the Temple, others, with good reason, highlight the fact that it is only the risen body of Jesus that

Jesus himself identifies with the Sanctuary of Israel (cf, for example, U. Busse, p. 340).

The authors who have studied Jn 2:13-22 often refer to other similar texts in John's Gospel. A classic text is Jn 1:14: 'And the Word became flesh and dwelt among us...(ἐσκήνωσεν ἐν ἡμῖν)'. In this 'dwelling' can be seen an allusion to the divine presence among the Israelites in the Tabernacle before the building of the Temple. Another passage is Jn 1:51: the reference to Jacob's Ladder (on which, according to Gen 28:12, the angels ascended and descended): interpreted in a Christological sense, it would mean that the angels will ascend and descend upon the Son of Man. Another passage often quoted in connection with the identification of Jesus with the Jerusalem Temple is the intimation which Jesus gives to the Samaritan Woman at Jn 4:21ff: 'Woman, believe me, the hour is coming when neither on this mountain nor in Jerusalem will you worship the Father. You worship what you do not know; we worship what we know, for salvation is from the Jews. But the hour is coming, and now is, when the true worshipers will worship the Father in spirit and truth, for such the Father seeks to worship him'. Here is the announcement of a superseding of the worship offered to God in the Temple of Jerusalem because of the coming of Christ.

In the great controversies of Chapters 7-10 of John's Gospel we find further allusions to the new Temple (cf among the rest, the article by C. Umoh). One could think of the words of Jesus about the rivers of living water which will flow from his belly (Jn 7:37f): probably the passage alludes to the Fountain of the Temple which will be present once again in the New Jerusalem of the eschatological age (Ez 47). Precisely on the Feast of the dedication of the Temple (Jn 10:22), Jesus speaks of his union with the Father in being or acting (10:25-38). In the Passion narrative there is a coinciding between the death of Jesus and the slaughter of the Paschal lambs. This type of sacrifice will no longer be necessary in the future cult. The cleansing of the Temple could already be preparing for such a development.

Mary M. Coloe takes still further the identification of Jesus with the Temple. According to her thesis, Jesus would take on the position of the Temple after its historical destruction in AD 70. Similarly, the Christian community takes the place of Jesus as locus of the divine presence after his death, resurrection and ascension. Coloe's key text is Jn 14:2: 'In my Father's house are many mansions'. If this text is read in connection with the rest of the chapter, the group of disciples appears as the place of the divine presence just as Jesus was at one time the place of the divine presence of the Temple. This interpretation of Jn 14, however, is not without difficulty. First of all, the passage in Jn 2:13-22 does not envisage a substitution for the cult of the Jerusalem Temple but only proposes a reinterpretation of this cult and of the Sanctuary (cf J. H. Ulrichsen). Moreover, in Jn 14:2, Jesus speaks of 'mansions' in his Father's house as a place for his disciples to live with God, not as the divine presence among men. The author of John 14 is referring to the ancient Christian tradition, inspired by apocalyptic Judaism, according to which God provides dwellings for the just in his own house. In the course of the chapter, this idea is developed in the sense of the dwelling of God and of Jesus among the faithful or in them, but in no way can it be said that the faithful take over the role of Jesus as the place of the divine presence.

3. *The Synagogue*

The term συναγωγή occurs only twice in John: at 6:59 and 18:20. In 18:20, the 'Synagogue' has been added to the 'Temple' as a place for the public teaching of Jesus. Perhaps the evangelist wanted to give more emphasis to this public teaching throughout the whole story of Jesus, not only at Jerusalem where he was arrested. A certain knowledge of the teaching of Jesus in the Synagogues of Galilee can be assumed on the part of the fourth evangelist

The case of Jesus' teaching in the Synagogue of Capernaum (Jn 6:59) remains exceptional. As we saw in the first lecture, the whole of Chapter 6 could have been added to the pre-existent gospel. The Passover mentioned in 6:4 frames the multiplication of the loaves, the crossing of the lake and the discourse of Jesus in the Synagogue of Capernaum in a Paschal context. However, Jesus does not seem to go up to Jerusalem to participate in the feast at the Temple. There are some reasons for supposing that the chapter reflects a situation in which the Jewish Passover has been replaced gradually by the Christian feast.

It is precisely in this chapter that John has inserted his Eucharistic discourse. It is only here that Jesus speaks of the necessity of eating his flesh and drinking his blood (Jn 6:51-8). In this sense, the Synagogue prefigures the future Christian place of assembly for the celebration of the Eucharist.

In John's Gospel, the Synagogue is always assumed to be a Jewish community. This appears clear from the three verses in which the concept ἀποσυνάγωγος is used (9:22; 12:42; 16:2). Chapter 9 speaks of a decision of the Jews to exclude from the Synagogue any person believing in Jesus. In 12:42, the evangelist mentions a powerful group of 'crypto-Christians' who believe in Jesus but do not have the courage to profess their faith for fear of being excluded from the Synagogue by the 'Pharisees' (probably the Sanhedrin). In 16:2, such an exclusion is promised to Jesus' followers after the departure of their Master. Probably these Johannine passages have undergone the influence of the period in which the Fourth Gospel was composed. From the book of J. L. Martyn, *History and Theology in the Fourth Gospel*,[7] the idea, which has become popular, is that this exclusion from the Synagogue reflects the decision taken by the so-called 'Synod of Jamnia' – towards the year AD 90 – to exclude Christians on the basis of the recitation of the Eighteen Benedictions. In these Benedictions there is found also a curse on the heretics, probably the Christians themselves. A Christian who was asked to recite this prayer would have refused to declaim it or else would have done it in an embarrassed way. Today, this ingenious proposal, based on the Babli Talmud.Ber 28b, has been abandoned. The identification of the 'minîm' (heretics) of b. Ber. 28b with the Christians is found only in a late manuscript. An exclusion of Christians *tout court* by the Synod of Jamnia cannot be proved, and it is even disputable whether this Synod had such great authority over all the Jewish communities of the Mediterranean.

What emerges from the three Johannine passages examined is that those Christians of the Johannine community who professed publicly their faith in Christ had to reckon with the possibility of exclusion from their Synagogue. For them, after he was healed, the man born blind

---

[7] New York – Evanston: Harper& Row, 1968.

would have been the anticipation of such an experience. He could have served as a role model for the disciples of later times, in the period of definitive separation between the Christians and the Jews who were organized in Synagogues.[8]

---

[8] Cf. J. BEUTLER, 'Faith and Confession: The Purpose of John,' in: J. PAINTER – R. A. CULPEPPER – F. F. SEGOVIA, ed., *Word, Theology, and Community in John*, St. Louis: Chalice Press 2002, 19-31.

Lecture IV

Scripture

Bibliography:

J. LUZÁRRAGA, 'Presentación de Jesús a la luz del A.T. en el Evangelio de Juan', *EE 51* (1976) 497-520; J. BEUTLER, 'The Use of "Scripture" in the Gospel of John', in: R. A. CULPEPPER, C. C. BLACK, ed., *Exploring the Gospel of John (FS D. M. Smith)*, Louisville, Kentucky: Westminster John Knox 1996, 147-162 = 'L'emploi de l'Écriture dans l'Évangile de Jean', *Transversalités. Revue de l'Institut Catholique de Paris 60* (Octobre-Décembre 1996) 133-153 = 'Der Gebrauch von "Schrift" im Johannesevangelium', in: Id., *Studien zu den johanneischen Schriften* (SBAB 25), Stuttgart: Katholisches Bibelwerk 1998, 295-315; M. J. J. MENKEN, *Old Testament Quotations in the Fourth Gospel: Studies in Textual Form*, [Kampen]: Kok Pharos 1996; PONTIFICAL BIBLICAL COMMISSION, *The Jewish People and its Sacred Scriptures in the Christian Bible*, Vatican City: Libreria Editrice Vaticana 2001; M. LABAHN, 'Jesus und die Autorität der Schrift im Johannesevangelium – Überlegungen zu einem spannungsreichen Verhältnis', in: ID. – K. SCHOLTISSEK – A. STROTMANN, ed., *Israel und seine Heilstraditionen im Johannesevangelium. Festgabe für Johannes Beutler SJ zum 70. Geburtstag*, Paderborn: Schöningh 2004, 185-206.

The sacred Scrptures of Israel – the *'Tanak'* (*Torah/Nebiim/ Ketubim*) were the 'Bible' of the first Christians. As for the first three evangelists and Paul, so also for John, the Sacred Scriptures of Israel were fundamental for the understanding and preaching of the Christian message. The fourth evangelist makes frequent recourse to the Scriptures of Israel. For a more detailed study of the connection betwen John's Gospel and the Scripture of Israel, it is necessary to distinguish between true and precise quotations and allusions that have various degrees of probablilty. When the study is limited to quotations, it is possible to make three observations which, at first sight, seem to have no connection: 1. The precise number of Old Testament quotations in

John remains open to discussion; 2. In many cases there is no certainty concerning the text form of the Scripture of Israel which has been adopted by the fourth evangelist as the basis for his text; 3. According to an increasing consensus (recently promoted, above all, by M. J. J. Menken), the Septuagint – the Greek version of the Tanak – was the chief textual base for the quotations in John's Gospel.

If these observations are taken together, we can formulate a first impression which can also serve us as a working hypothesis: John is less interested in the 'fulfilment' by Jesus of particular passages of the Old Testament than in the 'fulfilment' of Scripture as a whole (cf my article in the German edition,1998, p 297). This impression has been shared by various recent authors (including J. Luzárraga).

In what follows, we have confined our investigation to the passages in John's Gospel in which the evangelist uses the words 'Write' (γράφειν) or 'Scripture' (γραφή, γραφαι) with reference to the Sacred Scripture of Israel (without, however, including the *titulus* of the Cross as it is given in Jn 19:19-22). To this we have added some texts that speak of the 'fulfilment' of that which was spoken by the prophet Isaiah (Jn 1:23; 12;38, 39, 41).

We prescind from an exhaustive survey of the Old Testament quotations in John's Gospel. The most important and up-to-date contribution in this area is that of M. J. J. Menken, cited above. We prescind also from a detailed theological and Christological reflection as proposed by M. Labahn as a model. This author starts from the identification of Jesus with the eternal and divine Logos who enters into history as the mediator of creation and revelation. In Him, all the divine words find their fulfilment but also their boundary.

1. *The use of 'Scripture' and 'Write' in John*

The term γραφή is found twelve times in John. It always refers to the Scripture of Israel. The verb γράφειν is found twenty one times and, almost always with reference to 'Sacred Scripture' (plus an occurrence in the story which tells of Jesus' encounter with the Woman taken in Adultery in Jn 8:8 which we omit here).

Johannine verses with a more or les clear reference:

Jn 2:17 (the zeal of Jesus) refers clearly to Psalm 68:10 (LXX); the citation as 'Scripture' presupposes that the Psalms are considered as part of Scripture alongside the Law and the Prophets (cf Sir 39:1, and Preface; Lk 24:44);

Jn 6:45 seems to derive from Is 54:13 (LXX): the instruction of all by God; the introduction to the quotation remains unique in the New Testament: 'it stands written in the prophets';

Jn 10:34 ('you are gods') refers clearly to Psalm 81:6 (LXX); the introduction of the quotation as something that has been written in the 'Law' surprises, but further shows that the Psalms belong to 'Scripture'.

Jn 13:18 (the hand of the betrayer): once again a quotation taken from the Psalms (41:10 MT) is introduced as part of Scripture.

Jn 19:24 (the parting of Jesus' garments) is explained as the 'fulfilment' of Scripture, specifically of Psalm 21:19 (LXX);

Jn 19:37 is the only text in which γραφή signifies a particular quotation from Scripture, in this case Zcch 12:10 ('they shall look on me whom they have pierced');

In other cases, words of the prophet Isaiah are introduced as such:
Jn 1:23: Is 40:3 (LXX); Jn 12:38: Is 53:1 (LXX); Jn 12:39-41: Is 6:10 (LXX). In these three texts, the words of the prophet foretell Jesus or his harbinger, John the Baptist.

Johannine verses with an ambiguous reference to the Old Testament

Jn 6:31 ('He gave them bread from heaven to eat'). Here it is not clear if the reference to 'what is written' is to Ps 77:24 (LXX) or to another text such as Ex 16:4 or Ex 16:15;

Jn 7:37f remains obscure (cf Nestle-Aland: 'unde?'). A reference to the Temple fountain could have had an influence on the text;

Jn 7:42, the non-Galilean provenance of the Messiah recalls texts like 2 Sam 7:12; Ps 88:4f (LXX) or Jer 23:5 without its being possible to prefer one conclusively;

Jn 12:14f (Fear not, daughter of Zion...') combines various prophetic texts: Zech 9:9; Is 40:9; Zeph 3:14f.

Jn 12:16 takes up the same texts again but also others like Ps 118:25f (117.25f LXX);

Jn 15:25 ('They have hated me without a cause') does not have a clear Biblical reference; the text could be taken from Ps 34:19 (LXX) or Ps 68:5 (LXX).

Jn 17:12 (The betrayal of Judas) could refer to the tradition behind Jn 13:18 (above) or to other texts proposed by scholars;

Jn 19:28 ('I thirst') enjoys various scriptural explanations: Ps 68:22 (LXX); Ps 62:2 (LXX) or Ps 41:3 (LXX); we ought to note the formula 'to fulfil the Scripture perfectly', which looks as if it excels even the more usual 'so that the Scripture might be fulfilled'.

Jn 19:36 ('not a bone of him shall be broken') could refer to the Paschal Lamb according to Ex 12:10, 46; Num 9:12 or to the Suffering Righteous One in Ps 33:21 (LXX).

Johannine verses with reference to Moses or to the Law in general:

Jn 5:46 recounts that Moses wrote about Jesus, but the Johannine text does not say where he did this;

Jn 8:17 attributes to 'the Law' the principle that everything must be decided on the basis of two or three witnesses without giving the exact citation. The possible texts are Num 35:30 and Deut 17:6; 19:15.

Johannine verses with reference to Scripture as such:

In John's Gospel, we find texts according to which not only a particular Old Testament passage speaks of Jesus but the whole of the Scripture of Israel. A first example can be seen in Jn 1:45 where Philip says to Nathaniel: 'We have found him of whom Moses in the Law and also the prophets wrote'. On the basis of this Biblical message, Nathaniel can formulate his own confession of faith: 'Rabbi, you are the Son of God, you are the King of Israel' (1:49).

In two texts, John's Gospel supposes that the Resurrection of Jesus was pre-announced in the Scripture of Israel. According to Jn 2:22, it was only after Easter that the disciples were to understand the testimony of the Scriptures that He should rise from the dead. The passage of Scripture to which this conviction refers is not indicated. The same dilemma is presented in Jn 20:9: the two disciples who went running to the tomb and found it empty did not yet understand the Scripture that he must rise from the dead. Again, the text does not say which passage of Scripture is in question here. The impression is created that the whole of Scripture speaks of Jesus and of his Resurrection.

This impression is strengthened by another verse from John: 5:39. Debating with 'the Jews' of Jerusalem over his status, Jesus says to them: 'Search/You search the Scriptures because you think that in them you have eternal life; and it is they that bear witness to me'. There is not the hint of an explanation as to how and where the Scriptures bear witness to Jesus. According to John, the whole of Scripture speaks of Jesus when it is read with the understanding of faith.

The gospel put in written form

According to John's Gospel, the words of Jesus have not yet become Scripture, but they can be set down in written form and become authoritative like the words of the Scripture of Israel. In Jn 20:30f, the evangelist summarises the activity of Jesus, adding that Jesus did many other signs which are not written 'in this book' and reveals his purpose as author that the signs he has recounted may create faith in the readers, a faith which leads to eternal life. The entrusting of the gospel narration to written form becomes comparable to the 'Book' of the Bible without this making the gospel a part of the Bible of Israel. A similar passage is found in the second conclusion to the Fourth Gospel in Jn 21:24.

2. The words of Jesus and 'Scripture'

There are no reasons to suppose that the words of Jesus constitute part of Scripture for the fourth evangelist. It could be said, however, that these words have an authority comparable to that of Scripture. This is apparent in Jn 2:22: following the Cleansing of the Temple, there is a debate between Jesus and 'the Jews' over the rebuilding of the Temple, understood by Jesus as the resurrection of his own body. The disciples are not yet capable of understanding this message. It is only 'when he was raised from the dead, his disciples remembered that he had said this; and they believed the Scripture and the word which Jesus had spoken'.

A similar passage is found at the end of Jn 5. 'The Jews' are hostile to the message of Jesus although he has presented witnesses to support this message. Among others, he had also cited Moses and his writings. So Jesus concludes his discourse with the question: 'If you do not believe his writings, how will you believe my words?' Once again, the words of Jesus have an authority comparable to that of Moses' writings, without actually becoming 'Scripture'.

On the basis of this relationship, it can be said that, twice in John's Gospel, the words of Jesus are 'fulfilled': in Jn 18:9, a word from the Bread of Life Discourse which contains the request that none of those who have been entrusted to Jesus be lost (6:39); and in Jn 18:32 (at the point when Jesus is handed over to the Roman tribunal), the words in which are contained Jesus' announcement that the Son of Man must be lifted up. In such passages, Jesus' words are not yet part of 'Scripture'. Only as time goes on, the Fathers of the Church call them 'Scripture'.

3. 'Scripture' and Scripture

Up this point, we have pointed out that John's Gospel makes recourse to the Scripture of Israel, either with specific reference or in more global form. Beside those passages which refer to particular parts of the Old Testament, there are others which refer either to Moses (and the prophets) in general or to Scripture as a whole. It is appropriate to look at this phenomenon in a little more detail. A first observation is that the more general references to Scripture or to Moses are usually found on the lips of Jesus; the references to specific passages of the Old Testament, on the other hand, are found in comments by the evangelist. With few exceptions, the discourses of Jesus which contain references to Scripture as a whole are situated in the great controversies of Chapters 5-10 and the Farewell Discourses in Chapters 13-17. The evangelist's comments which refer to particular passages of the Old Testament are met with, on the other hand, in the Passion narrative in Jn 18-19.

Jesus' appeals to 'Scripture' in the great controversies

In these chapters we repeatedly come across the difficulty of indicating to what passage of Scripture's Reference by Jesus refers. It is the Scriptures as a whole that bear witness to Jesus (5:39). It is about Jesus that Moses has written (5:46). The words on the rivers of water flowing from Jesus (or from the believer?) do not match a clear reference to the Old Testament, and, moreover, the principle of the two witnesses necessary to establish something (8:17) is not quoted literally from the Book of Numbers or from Deuteronomy. In the dispute over the oneness of Jesus with the Father in Jn 10:32-38, a verse of a Psalm is quoted (81:6 LXX), but as part of Scripture the authority of which cannot be broken (10:35). The references to Scripture in Jn 6 are not found in an immediate context of controversy, but remain nonetheless imprecise (cf *supra* 1 with regard to Jn 6:31 and 6:45). Thus, the words of Philip to Nathaniel are to be read as a preannouncement of the standpoint of the following chapters: 'We have found him of whom Moses in the law and also the prophets wrote, Jesus of Nazareth' (1:45). For these central chapters of John, the witness of Scripture to Jesus is not to be found in this passage or that but in Scripture as a whole. It is enough to read it properly (i.e. from the Christian point of view).

Jesus' appeals to' Scripture' in the Farewell Discourses

In the Farewell Discourses, it is no longer the mission of Jesus that is announced in Scripture but his Passion; in these chapters too, it is often difficult to pin down the exact reference to Scripture. This goes for the prophecy of hatred of Jesus and his own 'without a cause' (Jn 15:25), but also for the promise that none of his own would be lost (Jn 17:12). Such passages presuppose Christian readers who understand the Scriptures as a witness to Jesus and his mission, even when there is no literal correspondence.

The evangelist's appeals to 'Scripture'

There are two passages in John's Gospel which speak of the Resurrection of Jesus on the third day as promised in Scripture (Jn 2:22 and 20:9) with a rather global reference. Beside these two texts, we find various comments of the evangelist which explain elements of Jesus' experience by appeal to specific Old Testament passages. These references are found, above all, in the Passion narrative (cf the already discussed reference to Zech 9:9 in the story of Jesus' Entry into Jerusalem (Jn 12:15). Almost all the other references are found in the account of the death of Jesus on the cross. As introductory formula, we have, repeatedly, the words: 'to fulfil the words', a formula utilized for the first time in Jn 12:38 and taken up again in Jn 19:24 (the parting of the garments of Jesus); cf also the similar but emphatic formula in Jn 19:28 (the thirst of Jesus) and the vents after the death of Jesus (Jn 19:36f). In these passages, John is seen to be nearer to the Synoptic tradition and shares with them the preoccupation of seeing all the details of the Passion witnessed to and preannounced in Scripture. In this way, the death of Jesus is shown to be willed by God because foretold in Scripture.

Lecture V

The Torah

Bibliography:

J. BEUTLER, *Martyria.Traditionsgeschichtliche Untersuchungen zum Zeugnisthema bei Johannes* (FTS 10), Frankfurt am Main: Knecht 1972; S. PANCARO, *The Law in the Fourth Gospel: The Torah and the Gospel, Moses and Jesus, Judaism and Christianity according to John* (NT.S. 42), Leiden: Brill 1975; J. BEUTLER, book review of Pancaro, *Bib.* 60 (1979) 144f.; M. KOTILA, *Umstrittener Zeuge – Studien zur Stellung des Gesetzes in der johanneischen Theologiegeschichte* (AASF), Helsinki: Suomalainen Tiedeakatemia 1988; J. BEUTLER, *Habt keine Angst. Die erste johanneische Abschiedsrede (Joh 14)*, (SBS 116), Stuttgart: Katholisches Bibelwerk 1984; J. AUGENSTEIN, '"Euer Gesetz" – Ein Pronomen und die johanneische Haltung zum Gesetz', *ZNW 88* (1997) 311-313; J. BEUTLER, 'Das Hauptgebot im Johannesevangelium,' in: ID., *Studien zu den johanneischen Schriften* (SBAB 25), Stuttgart: Katholisches Bibelwerk 1998, 107-120; ID., 'μαρτυρέω κτλ.', *EDNT* II (1991) 389-391: 'μαρτυρία' ibid. 391-393; ID., 'Gesetz und Gebot in Evangelium und Briefen des Johannes,' in: J. M. MRÁZEK – S. BRODSKÝ – RUT DVOŘÁKOVÁ, ed., *EPITOAUTO. Studies in honour of Petr Pokorný on his sixty-fifth birthday*, Prague: Mlýn 1998, 9-22; J. AUGENSTEIN, 'Jesus und das Gesetz im Johannesevangelium,' *Kirche und Israel* 14,2 (1999) 161-179.

Let us take, as the guide line for our discussion, the article written for the Festschrift for Petr Pokorný. This article is based on our work for the 2001 document of the Pontifical Biblical Commission (*The Jewish People and its Sacred Scriptures in the Christian Bible*).

1. *The 'Law' in John's Gospel*

The term νόμος occurs fifteen times in John's Gospel; almost always with the definite article (with the exception of Jn 19:7: 'we have *a* law'). In every case, the term refers to the Mosaic Law. We must note, however, the semantic difference between the original Hebrew *torah* and its Greek translation νόμος: the Hebrew word derives from the root *jrh* and signifies 'instruction' rather than 'law'.

Generally speaking, it is the Jews or Jesus who speak of the Law in the Fourth Gospel, the exception to the rule being in Jn 18:31 where Pilate says: 'Take him and judge him according to your law'. The Jews speak of the Law in 7:49; 12:34; 19:7 (cf 7:51) while Jesus does so in 7:19, 23; 8:17; 10:34; 15:25. From both points of view the word 'law' is cited with argumentative force in the controversies about Jesus. Exegetes discuss whether the expression 'your law', used by Jesus in 8:17; 10:34; cf 15:25, signifies that Jesus is assuming a distance from the Torah. J. Augenstein shows, with justification, that this adjective ('your') does not signify distance because Jesus puts himself on the same level of argument as his adversaries: in the two cases in Jn 8 and John 10, he is referring to a text of Scripture. In two cases it is the disciples who speak of the 'law'. In Jn 1:45, Philip bears witness to Jesus as he of whom the Law and the prophets have spoken (cf *supra* Lecture 4); in Jn 1:17f, the Law on the one hand and the grace and truth brought by Jesus Christ on the other are set in opposition. However, this passage of the Prologue has caused huge discussion. It seems preferable to see in the parallelism between verse 17 and 18 not an antithesis but a climax (cf also J. Augenstein, *Kirche und Israel*). The two verses are in fact explaining the twofold χάριν ἀντὶ χάριτος of v 16 (Augenstein). Both the Law of Moses and the revelation of Jesus are gifts of the divine grace. Both forms of revelation have the same source: the Divine Logos who had already inspired Moses.

Semantics: The term νόμος is used with a double sense in John: either as the Mosaic legislation proper or as 'Scripture' (or as part of it). The concept is used in its first sense by 'the Jews' when they speak against Jesus during his trial by the Romans (Jn 19:7). Pilate is able to follow suit (Jn 18:31). In the controversies over the Sabbath, Jesus refers to the 'law' of Moses (Jn 7:19, 23) to justify his actions. Also, in the controversy between Nicodemus and the other members of the Sanhedrin, the compatibility between Jesus' activity and the Law of Moses is discussed (Jn 7:49, 51). In Jn 8:17 we come across the other meaning of νόμος, that of 'Scripture'. The discussion concerns the principle whereby for any decision, in a judicial dispute, two witnesses are necessary. The context is Christological. In 10:34, a quotation taken from a Psalm can be spoken of as 'law': Ps 82:6. Once again the question of who Jesus is stands at the centre of the debate. Similarly, in Jn 15:25, Jesus refers to the Psalms as 'law'; they have foretold the fate of Jesus and his own of being hated without a cause by all. It is clear, then, that the concept of 'law' in John is used, whether in its strictly juridical sense or in its wider sense as 'Scripture', predominantly as a means of argument in the Christological controversies of the Fourth Gospel. The verses that speak of Moses or of the Scriptures as 'witnesses' to Jesus (Jn 5:39, 46f) are part of this perspective.

Pragmatics: the use of 'law' in John can be understood if set in the context of the controversies over Jesus at the end of the first century. In the disputes recounted in the Synoptic Gospels, the discussion is still concerned with details of interpretation of the Mosaic legislation such as the purity of hands and vessels (Mk 7:1-23 par), fasting (Mk 2:18-22 or the plucking of the ears of corn on the Sabbath (Mk 2:23-27 par). In John, more strongly than in the Synoptic Gospels, the person and the mission of Jesus stand at the centre of the debate. The fourth evangelist writes at a time in which the Church and the Synagogue are already separated. The decisive question is whether Christ is the Messiah promised to Israel, and the Son of God in a somewhat qualified sense. In the last resort, all the appeals to Scripture are ancillary to this debate. In the course of his narrative, the fourth evangelist presents his readers with examples of courageous decision made for faith in Christ, such as Nicodemus and the man born blind. The reader must learn to choose between receiving glory from men or from God (cf 5:41-44; 7:18; 12:41-43)[9].

The most severe controversy, in Jn 8:31-59, is to be explained against the background of this historical situation. As is clear from the beginning of this section (Jn 8:30), Jesus is addressing himself to those Jews who had come to believe in him. They have to remain faithful to their decision of faith in order not to become 'children of the devil'. Far from being a judgement on the Jews, this passage is directed to

---

[9] On this aspect, cf JB in *GuL* 76 (2003) 83-91.

Christian readers in order that they may remain faithful to their vocation and persevere in their faith.

Up until now, we have been reading the Johannine texts in a 'synchronic' way. M. Kotila reads them under a 'diachronic' aspect, distinguishing four phases of development in the relations between the Jews and the Christians of the Johannine community: from a situation in which Christians are still part of the Synagogue and discuss problems of *halakhah* such as Sabbath observance, to the separation and exclusion of Christians from the Synagogue, up to the almost total estrangement of the two communities at the moment of the redaction of the Johannine Letters. However, this reconstruction remains hypothetical, strongly based on the distinction between the sources made by Bultmann.

2. *The 'Commandment' in John's Gospel*

The use of the word ἐντολή, 'commandment', and of the corresponding verb ἐντέλλομαι, 'command', corresponds in large measure to that of νόμος, 'law', 'instruction'. These ideas, which have their roots in the Old Testament, have been Christianised. In one particular case, the word ἐντολή has a significance which is not religious, indicating an arrest warrant (Jn 11:57). In the other cases, the word has a religious character.

In a first series of passages, Jesus speaks of the 'commandment' which he has received from the Father to pursue his course to the very depths (Jn 10:18; 12:49f; 14:31). In a second series of passages, the 'commandment' is that of the mutual love of the disciples; in this context we also find the verb 'command (cf Jn 13:34; 15:12, 17). In other, similar, passages, Jesus speaks of his 'commandments' in the plural (14:15, 21; 15:10). As we shall see, these passages belong to another cultural and theological background.

The first series of passages is founded on the will of God the Father which his Son follows. This is his path to the end. A first passage which speaks of this necessity is that of the Cleansing of the Temple (Jn 2:19-22). In the Good Shepherd Discourse, Jesus' readiness to remain faithful to his vocation and mission, and so to the 'commandment' of the Father, is expressed by means of his readiness to give his life for those who are his own (Jn 10:18). In obedience to this 'commandment' of the Father, Jesus 'rises up' in the course of the Last Supper and goes towards his Passion (Jn 14:31). This obedience in his relations with the Father is at the same time an expression of Jesus' love for his own to the end or to the utmost (Jn 13:1). This love can also be expressed as the gift of his own life for his friends (Jn 15:12f).

The commandment of mutual love of the disciples for one another (the second series of passages) finds its root and reason in the love of Jesus for his own (Jn 13:34f; 15:12-17). The fourth evangelist is basing himself here on the command of love of neighbour (according to the reference to Lev 19:18), but also the taking up of this commandment in the Synoptic tradition (Mk 12:31 par; Rom 13:9). But in contrast with Lev 19, the Synoptic passages and Paul, John does not speak of love of the 'neighbour' but of the 'brother'. The difference should not be exaggerated given that the רֵעַ of which Leviticus speaks is the fellow national and brother in the people of God, by contrast with the πλησίον of the LXX and the New Testament which signifies simply the 'neighbour', even in a physical sense. This is something that receives little attention in the commentaries and monographs on the theme of love in John.

The third group of Johannine texts which speak of the 'commandments' is constituted by the words which Jesus pronounces at the Last Supper. In John 14:15-24, Jesus exhorts his own to love him and to keep his 'commandments'. If the disciples keep this exhortation, Jesus will send them the Holy Spirit from the Father. He himself will come with the Father to find a dwelling place among the disciples or within them. In my study of Jn 14, I sought to show that this vocabulary goes back to the Decalogue and to Deuteronomy where 'to love' God and 'to keep' his 'commandments' are part of the theology of the Covenant. Cf Deut 7:9 – 'Know therefore that the LORD your God is God, the faithful God who keeps covenant and steadfast love with those who love him and keep his commandments, to a thousand generations...'.

It would seem that the fourth evangelist has taken up this theology of the Covenant to integrate it with the perspective of the New Covenant foretold by the prophets, particularly by Jeremiah (31:31-34) and Ezekiel (36-37). Thus, God will make his dwelling among and within his people (Ez 37:27). He will give them his Spirit (Ez 36:26). The disciples will receive the eschatological promises of the Holy Spirit, justice, peace and joy (cf Jn 14:25-29; 16:4b-33; 20:19-23), that constitute the kingdom of God (cf Rom 14:17). With regard to the vocabulary of love and of keeping the commandments, this has its roots in the most ancient traditions of the Old Testament and even of the ancient Orient (with the vassal treaty formulae): in this way, therefore, the fourth evangelist appears particularly archaic in his mode of thinking and of expressing himself.

3. The 'chief commandment' of the love of God in John

In my article 'Das Hauptgebot im Johannesevangelium' I have shown that the New Testament speaks almost exclusively of the love of God with reference to the' chief commandment' to love God according to Deut 6:4-13, the $\check{S}^e ma'$ Israel. The principal passages are: Mk 12:28-32 parr, Mt 4:10//Lk 4:8; Lk 11:42; Mt 24:12; in Paul: Rom 8:28; 1 Cor 2:9 (with the participial style of the Decalogue), 1 Cor 8:3 (reference to the uniqueness of God in the following verse), then 2 Thess 3:5 and Jas 1:12; 2:5.

All the other passages of the New Testament which speak of the love of God are found in the Johannine corpus. We confine our attention here to John's Gospel; for the Letters, cf especially the article and commentary of 2000 (RNT).

Jn 5:41-44: in this passage, Jesus contrasts two ways of living: one can seek one's own glory, referring to men and placing one's trust in one's own name or else one can seek to love the only God and to receive from him true glory. Against the background of this structure, it appears that 'the love of God' in v 42 is clearly the love that man has for God and not the love with which God loves men (objective not subjective genitive). It is right to detect behind this semantic field that of the 'chief commandment' of Deut 6:4ff. Decisive proof for this reading is found in the fact the concept of the love of God appears in connection with that of his uniqueness. Further confirmation is found in the verses which form the frame of vv 41-44: in vv 39f, Jesus invites 'the Jews' to search the Scriptures (of Moses, evidently) and to find the witness of these writings to Jesus. In vv 45-47, Jesus returns to the figure of Moses. It is he who accuses 'the Jews' because they refuse to believe in the Jesus of whom he has written.

Jn 8:41f: the same semantic field of the love and uniqueness of God recurs in Jn 8:41f. In this case, it is the love shown for Jesus as the one sent from God. 'The Jews' declare that they have 'a Father', that is God. Jesus challenges this declaration because 'the Jews' would have also to love Jesus who comes from God. The idea is clear: either one loves the true and only God, and in this case also him who has been sent by that God, or one refuses this twofold love and remains in unbelief (sons of adultery).

Jn 14:15-24: an echo of the 'chief commandment' can be found in Jn 14:15-24. As has been seen, the vocabulary of this passage is firmly based on that of the Book of Deuteronomy. We find present together the concept of 'loving' (Jesus) and of 'keeping his commandments' in connection with the eschatological promises of the New Covenant. As in Deuteronomy (7:8; 10:15), the love of God corresponds to that of Israel and precedes it, so also the love of God for the disciples corresponds to the love of the disciples for Jesus in Jn 14:15-24 (14:21, 23).

Jn 21:15-17: for one last time, the theme of the love of Jesus is taken up in the post-Easter scene of Jn 21:15-17. Peter has denied the Lord three times. Now the Lord poses the question to him three times: 'Do you love me?' In Chapter 6, Peter had been the spokesman for the faith of the band of disciples, saying: 'Lord, to whom shall we go? You have the words of eternal life; and we have believed, and have come to know, that you are the Holy One of God' (6:68f). To this confession of faith that was subsequently denied we see the correspondence of that of Peter by the Sea of Galilee. Like the *Š͏ᵉmaʿ Israel*, Peter's confession is at one and the same time a confession of love as well as faith. Peter renews his fundamental relationship with Jesus and, at the same time, with God: because of this, he will be able to be accepted once again as a disciple of Jesus and will be destined to follow him to the death so as to share one day also in his Resurrection (Jn 21:18f).

Lecture VI

The Prophets

Bibliography:

J. BEUTLER, *Habt keine Angst. Die erste johanneische Abschieds-rede (Joh 16)* (SBS 116), Frankfurt a. M.: Knecht 1984; ADELE REINHARTZ, 'Jesus as Prophet. Predictive prolepses in the Fourth Gospel,' *JSNT* 36 (1989) 3-16; P. TRUDINGER, 'A prophet like me (Deut. 18:15). Jesus and Moses in St John's gospel, once again,' *DR* 113 (1995) 193-195.

Alongside the 'Law', the Prophets play an important role in John's Gospel. By contrast with the Jewish and Rabbinic tradition, the New Testament in general and the Fourth Gospel in particular attribute a particular importance to the prophets of Israel. In this lecture, the concept of 'prophet' is taken in the Christian sense (as God's messenger to the People of Israel whose writings have been preserved), without any reference to Moses and the so-called 'historical' books of the Old Testament (from Joshua up to the Books of Kings). We shall speak initially of the prophets in general in the Fourth Gospel; then of some prophets who are named explicitly; in the third place, we shall look at prophetic traditions used in the Fourth Gospel, and, in conclusion at Jesus himself as prophet according to John.

1. *'The Prophets' in the Fourth Gospel*

In some passages, the Fourth Gospel speaks of 'the Prophets' in general. In the first passage, the Jewish understanding of the concept seems to be presupposed. In Jn 8:31-58, Jesus finds himself involved in a fierce controversy with 'the Jews' of Jerusalem over his prerogatives. In v 51, Jesus promises that all those who keep his words shall not die. This declaration arouses indignation among his hearers because it implies that he considers himself immortal. So they say: 'Abraham died, as did the prophets; and you say, `If any one keeps my word, he will never taste death.' Are you greater than our father Abraham, who died? And the prophets died! Who do you claim to be?' (Jn 8:52f). Abraham had already been mentioned. The prophets are those who have addressed God's word to the people. If they have died, it is legitimate to expect that Jesus too is mortal, and, *a fortiori*, those to whom he has addressed his words. Jesus does not accept the logic of this, and bases the legitimacy of his claim on the fact that he is not seeking his own glory but that of the Father. Because of this he too is glorified by God and shares in the eternity of God so that he existed before Abraham (8:58). This claim is again rejected: 'the Jews' take up stones to throw at him for blasphemy.

In two other passages, the 'prophets' constitute part of the Scripture of Israel. After his first meeting with Jesus, Philip says to Nathaniel: 'We have found him of whom Moses in the law and also the prophets wrote, Jesus of Nazareth, the son of Joseph.' (Jn 1:45). This text belongs to that group of passages in the Fourth Gospel which assume that the whole of Scripture speaks of Jesus (cf, *supra*, Lecture 4). It is not specified in any way how or where Moses and the prophets spoke of Jesus. A 'Christian' reading of the sacred books of Israel seems to be presupposed.

The second passage in question is Jn 6:45. Jesus quotes a prophetic text with the introduction: 'It is written in the prophets: They will all be taught of God'. The text to which Jesus is referring is to be found in Is 54:13 or in Jer 31:34. This lack of precision in citation is noted also by the commentators. For John it is not so important what prophet pronounced such and such a prophecy. More important is the witness of all the prophets to Jesus and his promises.

2. *The 'prophet' Isaiah in the Fourth Gospel*

The only prophet cited under his own name in the Fourth Gospel is Isaiah. It could be said that the passages which are attributed to him form a framework into which the whole of the Fourth Gospel that speaks of the public life of Jesus before his passion is fitted (Jn 1-12).

The first passage comes in Jn 1:23. John the Baptist has begun his activity in the Jordan Valley. Immediately this causes apprehension on the part of the Jewish authorities in Jerusalem who send a delegation to see who the Baptist is and what he is up to. John denies that he is the Messiah or Elijah or the eschatological prophet. To the question who he is, therefore, he replies: 'I am the voice of one crying in the wilderness, 'Make straight the way of the Lord,' as the prophet Isaiah said'. The text presupposes the Septuagint reading of Is 40:3. In the original Hebrew text, the expression 'in the desert' refers to the region in which the way of the Lord is to be prepared. In the Septuagint and in the Gospels (cf Mk 1:2 par; Mt 3:3; Lk 3:4) on the other hand, this expression is associated with the one who cries: so it becomes applicable to John the Baptist. For the fourth evangelist, Isaiah has foreseen and foretold the work of the Baptist as the work of the one who is preparing the way of the Lord, identified in our Gospel as in the Synoptics, with Jesus.

The other explicit citation of the 'prophet' Isaiah is found in Jn 12:38. The verse is part of a section in which 'Isaiah' is named as many as three times. In 12:38 Isaiah is used to account for the fact that the Jews have not believed in Jesus (cf Is 53:1). In 12:39, he is used to explain why they were not able to believe in him (cf Is 6:10). In 12:40, Isaiah is named for a third time. He was able to foretell Jesus and the fate of his preaching because he had seen his glory (cf Is 6:1; the divine apparition at the beginning of Isaiah's prophetic career is interpreted as a vision of Christ). Once again we see how the Christian reading of the prophets determines their interpretation.

This repeated occurrence of citations of the prophet Isaiah in the same chapter and indeed in the same paragraph of John is interesting. In fact, as I have sought to show in a lecture at the Pontifical Biblical Institute in 1990, Isaiah seems to dominate the whole section Jn 12:20-43.[10] The desire of 'the Greeks' to see Jesus could derive from Is 52:15 in the LXX reading (cf Rom 15:21). The exaltation and glorification of Jesus according to Jn 12:20-36 seems to derive from Is 52:13, the first verse of the Fourth Servant Song (LXX). The suffering of the Servant and his glorification and exaltation are the great themes of this section of John; only the title of 'Servant' has been replaced by that of 'Son of Man'. It could be said that Jn 12:20-43 is a sort of 'midrash' of Isaiah,

---

[10] 'Greeks come to see Jesus (John 12,20f.)', *Bibl.* 71 (1990) 333-347 = ID., 'Griechen kommen, um Jesus zu sehen (Joh 12,20f.)', in: ID., *Studien zu den johanneischen Schriften* (SBAB 25), Stuttgart: Katholisches Bibelwerk 1998, 175-189.

written from a Christian perspective in the light of Easter after the death and resurrection of Jesus.

If we consider again the possibility that the whole of the public life of Jesus in John is framed with quotations taken from the prophet Isaiah, it is worth also taking into account the testimony of John the Baptist at the beginning of the Gospel after the encounter with the Jewish authorities sent from Jerusalem: 'Behold the Lamb of God' (Jn 1:29, 36). Various suggestions have been made to explain the nature of this testimony. The most probable remains that which interprets the Baptist's words in the light of the Fourth Servant Song where there occurs the image of the sheep which suffers in silence (Is 53:7) and the idea of the substitutionary death of the Servant for the sins of many. If this interpretation is valid, Jn 1-12 is framed not only by the prophet Isaiah in general but by the figure of the Servant foretold by Isaiah in particular.

3. *Prophetic Traditions used in the Fourth Gospel*

In the fourth lecture, we made a list of the Old Testament quotations in John's Gospel. From this it appears that the majority of the quotations obtained from the prophets are taken from the Book of Isaiah. Among the other prophets, Zechariah stands out, more precisely Deutero-Zechariah (Zech 9-14). This prophet is quoted in the account of the Entrance of Jesus into Jerusalem (cf the combination of Zech 9:9; Is 40:9; Zeph 3:14f in Jn 12:14f). Of particular interest is the use of Zech 12:10 in the scene where Jesus' side is piereced according to Jn 19:37 ('they shall look on me whom they have pierced').

In my study of 1984, *Habt keine Angst. Die erste johanneische Abschiedsrede (Joh 14)*, I sought to show how in vv 25-29 of Chapter 14 there is a theology of the eschatological promises of the prophets. Jesus is on the point of departing. His own will remain united to him in faith (vv 4-14). He will return among his own, united with him in love, and will make his dwelling within or among them, together with the Father and the Holy Spirit (cf vv 15-24). Behind this promise stands the theology of the (New) Covenant as I have sought to demonstrate (cf also above, the fifth lecture).

In verses 25-29 we find a triple promise by Jesus: he promises to his own the gift of the Holy Spirit (v 26). Then he declares to his own that he is leaving them his peace (v 27). In conditional form, he speaks of the joy which the disciples can have if they love him (v 28). These themes are taken up again in Jn 16:4b-33 where, at the moment of farewell, Jesus promises his own peace (v 33), joy (vv 19-22), justice (vv 8-11) and the Holy Spirit (vv 7-15). On Easter Day, Jesus appears among his own (Jn 20:19-23) and greets them with the greeting of peace (vv 19, 21). The disciples are full of joy (v 20). Then Jesus breathes on them and says: 'Receive the Holy Spirit' (v 22).

As I have tried to show, behind these promises lies a synthesis of those eschatological promises which Paul, on his part, synthesises with the expression 'Kingdom of God': 'For the kingdom of God is not food and drink but righteousness and peace and joy in the Holy Spirit' (Rom 14:17).

These eschatological promises find their basis in the prophetic tradition of the Old Testament. Above all, the complex 'justice, peace and joy' comes from a royal tradition which has its roots in the ancient Orient, in the hymns that were sung on the occasion of the accession to the throne of the kings and the emperors of the great kingdoms of the Middle East. In Israel, this divine kingship is generally denied to human kings and reserved to God himself (cf the Psalms of Kingship, especially Pss 93-99 where the kingship of God is hymned with praise for the justice which emanates from God and for the joy which the children of Israel feel). In the Exilic and post-Exilic age, this kingdom of justice and joy becomes, together with peace, the expectation of the people for the eschatological and messianic future. The Exilic and post-Exilic prophets speak of this time and first of all, Trito-Isaiah together with some late passages inserted into the first part of Isaiah (1-39): cf the promise of a future reign of justice and peace in Is 2:1-5 and the 'nativity' text of Is 11:1-9 where too there is promised the dwelling of the Spirit of God on his Anointed One. In Deutero-Isaiah (40-55), the promises of the return of Israel to its land and of future joy and freedom predominate. In Trito-Isaiah (56-66), the horizon is broadened. The nations too participate in the salvation of Israel (cf the promises of a future peace, justice and joy in Is 61 and the description of the New

Zion in Is 62). The promise of a peaceful future in which 'the wolf and the lamb shall feed together, the lion shall eat straw like the ox; and dust shall be the serpent's food' is found in Is 65 (v 25). The same theme is taken up again in the last chapter of the book (66). The joy of the people of God (vv 66, 10f) will be accompanied and inspired by the peace gifted by God (v 12). The Lord will execute judgement (v 16). John is inspired by all these promises in his Farewell Discourses and in the Easter narrative.

The gift of the Holy Spirit finds its Biblical basis above all in the prophecy of the 'New Covenant' in Ez 36:26f.

4. *Jesus as prophet in John*

At the beginning of the Gospel, John too has material concerning the identity of the Baptist. According to the Fourth Gospel, John the Baptist denies that he is the Messiah, or Elijah or 'the Prophet'. Scholars discuss to what prophet this denial refers (in Jn 1:25, cf 21). The most accepted suggestion is that which sees in the syntagm 'the prophet' a reference to the figure foretold by Moses in Deut 18:18: 'I will raise up for them a prophet like you from among their brethren; and I will put my words in his mouth, and he shall speak to them all that I command him'. The same tradition from Deuteronomy could have had an influence on the judgement of the crowd in Jerusalem during the Feast of Tabernacles: This is really the prophet' (Jn 7:40). Already in this text the alternative would be to see in Jesus the Messiah (v 41f). Messianic traits are also found in the judgement of the witnesses of the multiplication of loaves in Jn 6:14: 'This is indeed the prophet who is to come into the world'. According to W. A. Meeks[11] there is present also here the influence of Mosaic traditions on this Johannine text. In other Johannine texts, Jesus is described simply as 'a prophet'. Such a description appears to be one of the steps along the road to faith of people to whom Jesus reveals himself progressively. Take the case of the Samaritan Woman who comes to the conclusion: 'Sir, I perceive that you are a prophet' (Jn 4:19). The same thing

---

[11] *The Prophet-King. Moses-Traditions and Johannine Christology* (NT.S 14), Leiden: Brill 1967.

happens with the judgement of the man born blind: 'He is a prophet' (Jn 9:17). In both passages, the person to whom Jesus reveals himself comes to a deeper confession. In the end, the Samaritan Woman asks: 'Can this be the Christ?' (4:29), and when he has been healed, the man born blind replies to Jesus' question: 'Do you believe in the Son of Man?' with the words: 'Lord, I believe', and worships him (Jn 9:35-38). And it is Jesus who applies to himself the saying: 'a prophet has no honour in his own country' (Jn 4:44). According to the members of the Sanhedrin, no prophet is to come from Galilee (Jn 7:52). From this list of references, it is evident that Jesus appears as a prophet in John's Gospel, even as *the* Prophet', but this title does not exhaust his dignity. He is also the Messiah, the Son of man foretold by Daniel (Dan 7:14) and the Son of God, or simply 'the Son' (cf Jn 3:3-18).

According to the Jewish author, A. Reinhartz, Jesus appears continually in the Fourth Gospel as a prophet. It is possible to distinguish prolepses that are internal, external and uncertain. Internal prolepses are those which are realised within the narrative, the external ones, those which are realised outside the narrative, while the uncertain ones leave open the moment of their realization (according to the author, for example, we are concerned with passages in which Jesus foretells an event for the moment of 'the hour'). As far as the literary aspect is concerned, the prophecies serve in the interests of the plot; in other words, in the interests of the unity of the narrative.[12]

The ability to predict the future is the sign by which the true prophet like Moses can be recognised according to Deut 18:15-18. At this point there come together the traditions regarding prophets in general and the prophet like Moses.

---

[12] cf. A. R. CULPEPPER, *Anatomy of the Fourth Gospel*, Philadelphia: Fortress 1983.

Lecture VII

The Sapiential Tradition

Bibliography:

THOMAS H. TOBIN, 'The Prologue of John and Hellenistic Jewish Speculation', *CBQ* 52 (1990) 252-269; J. BEUTLER, 'Johannes-Evangelium (u.–Briefe)', *RAC* XVIII *(1998)* 646-670 (with A. MEREDITH): 656-659.

Not all the Wisdom Books of the Old Testament have had an important influence on John's Gospel. The contacts with the Book of Job remain sporadic. The same goes for Qoheleth. The contacts with the Song of Songs are more numerous. These have been studied by J. Luzárraga and Sandra C. Schneiders among others. The passages that have been particularly studied are the anointing of Jesus in the house of Martha and Mary (Jn 12:1-8) and the encounter between Jesus and Mary Magdalen on Easter morning (Jn 20:1-2, 11-18). We shall look at the Psalms in the next lecture.

There is a noteworthy literary contact between some passages of Proverbs, Wisdom of Solomon and Sirach, on the one hand, and the Prologue of John on the other.

1. *The Prologue of John (Jn 1:1-18) and the Wisdom Tradition*

We might make a kind of abstract speculation on the problem if we were to make out a hymn, Christian or (as Bultmann thought) pre-Christian, behind the Prologue of John. Many contemporary scholars suppose such hymn in praise of the Logos in vv 1-5, 10-12b and 14, 16, taking as redactional additions the verses regarding John the Baptist (6-8 or 6-9 and 15) and those which make the comparison between the revelation made in Moses and in Jesus Christ (vv 17-18). In fact, the origin and the destiny of the Logos are described in vv 1-5 and 9-12 with the conclusion in 14 and 16: what is described is the heavenly origin of the divine Logos, his coming among men and his destiny, a destiny which demands an attitude of refusal or acceptance. This scheme finds its antecedents in the Sapiential texts of the Old Testament which speak of the mission of Divine Wisdom. It is possible to distinguish two forms of a similar typology:

A) The first type takes its starting point from the idea of the pre-existence of Wisdom which is given as presupposed.

Pr 8:22-36: 'The LORD created me at the beginning of his work, the first of his acts of old. Ages ago I was set up, at the first, before the beginning of the earth' (22f). Expression is given to a certain participation by Wisdom in the creative work of God: 'Then I was beside him, like a master workman; and I was daily his delight...' (30). At the end, we find an invitation to men to accept the Divine Wisdom sent by God with a promise of happiness and life, and, conversely, a threat of death for those who do not accept such a Divine Messenger (32-36).

Wisd 9:9f: 'With you is Wisdom, she who knows your works, she who was present when you made the world; she understands what is pleasing in your eyes and what agrees with your commandments. Despatch her from the holy heavens, send her forth from your throne of glory to help me and to toil with me and teach me what is pleasing to you.' This is the prayer of 'Solomon'.

Sir 24:1-21: Divine Wisdom pervades the world but makes its dwelling place in Israel. 'From eternity, in the beginning, he created me, and for eternity I shall not cease to exist. In the holy tabernacle I ministered before him, and so I was established in Zion. In the beloved city likewise he gave me a resting place, and in Jerusalem was my dominion' (9ff). At the end, again, there is an invitation to acceptance (18-21).

B) In a second type, the pre-existence of Wisdom is not presupposed:

Wisd 6:12-16: After praise of Wisdom we find a description of her searching for those who accept her: 'she goes about seeking those worthy of her, and she graciously appears to them in their paths, and meets them in every thought' (16).

Wisd 7:22-8:1: In this passage too, Wisdom is praised for a spirit that is penetrating and benevolent towards men. Wisdom comes from God, 'she is a breath of the power of God, and a pure emanation of the glory of the Almighty' (7:25). She is called 'an image of his goodness' (26), and 'she renews all things' (27). 'She reaches mightily from one end of the earth to the other, and she orders all things well' (8:1).

However, the similarity of such passages with John's Prologue has its limits as Tobin (*op cit*) has shown:
    – the sapiential texts speak of 'Wisdom' not of the Divine Logos;
    – there is no claim to creation by means of (διά) the Logos or Wisdom as is made in the Prologue;
    – the sapiential texts lack the dualistic opposition between 'light' and 'darkness' typical of the Prologue;
    – they also lack the promise of 'life' associated with the acceptance of Wisdom or the Logos (but the text of Prov 8 cited above should be noted).

2. *The development of the Wisdom Tradition in Hellenistic Judaism*

The tradition of the Wisdom that goes in search of men was developed above all by Philo of Alexandria (cf Tobin, *op cit*). In Philo, Wisdom appears as the 'Logos'. This concept has been developed by Philo under a dual influence: that of the Stoic doctrine of the 'Logos' as the rational principle pervading the world, and that of the Platonic concept of the 'Logos' – as world soul – according to Plato's account in his *Timaeus*. However, Philo also takes up the influence of the Biblical tradition and develops his doctrine of the Logos while commenting on the Pentateuch, above all the biblical account of the Creation in Gen 1-3. The notion of the participation of the Logos in the work of creation could also come from Middle Platonism. In so far as the Logos had an instrumental role in the work of creation, Philo goes beyond the Wisdom concept which is limited to attributing to Wisdom some role in the creative work of God. Parallels for this concept are found both in Rabbinical thought (the instrumental role of the Torah in creation – cf

'Abot 3,15) and in early Christianity (cf Jesus Christ as he 'through whom all things were created', Col 1:16f; cf 1 Cor 8:6).

In common with the Johannine Prologue, Philo has also the opposition between 'light' and 'darkness', the belonging of the Logos to 'the light' and the contribution of the Logos to the gift of 'life' (cf Tobin, 262-265). The text in which Philo comes nearest to the Johannine concept of the logos is *Opif.m.* 29-35. Here, the Logos is assigned by Philo to the first day of creation in which, together with the light, God creates the rational world; the world that can be perceived by the senses is created only on the second day. Just as the light is the image of the Logos who in his turn appears as image of God, so also the life-giving Spirit is of the divine nature, belongs to the invisible, incorporeal world and is, in the end, identical with the Logos. In Philo as in John, 'life' is understood is a very wide sense (cf Jn 1:3). Among other things, the Logos has, in Philo, also an anagogic function: it leads men to the knowledge and vision of God so that they can become the sons of God, or at least of the Logos (cf Tobin 260-262). However, it is still true that for Philo, the Logos remains a rational principle: the idea of the incarnation of the Logos in a human person would have been unthinkable for the Jew of Alexandria. This is to maintain a substantial difference between the Jewish thinker and the evangelist.

Lecture VIII

The Psalms. Psalm 42/3

Bibliography:

J. BEUTLER, '"Ich habe gesagt: Ihr seid Götter". Zur Argumentation mit Ps 82,6 in Joh 10,34-36', in: G. GÄDE, ed., *Hören – Glauben – Denken. FS P. Knauer* (Theologie. Forschung und Wissenschaft 14), Münster: LIT Verlag 2005, 101-113.

1. *The Psalms*

Besides the Pentateuch and the Prophets, the Psalms have a particularly important role to play in the Fourth Gospel. In the fourth lecture, we provided a list of quotations, taken from the Psalms, which are found in the Fourth Gospel. A first observation is that the majority of the quotations occur in the context of the Passion. Quotations drawn from the Psalms are rare in the first part of the Gospel. In Jn 10:34, Jesus refers to a verse of Psalm 82 (82:6): 'I have said: "You are gods, sons of the Most High, all of you"', to affirm his character of being divine in nature or Son of God. According to the most accepted interpretation, these words of the Lord refer to the Israelites, and as a result of this, Jesus can find common ground with his audience. The Jewish tradition, in fact, understands the verse as words of Yahweh directed to the people of God at Sinai: to the extent that they listen to his voice and are obedient to him, they can be called gods and sons of the Most High; if, however, they become unfaithful (as in the incident of the golden Calf), they will hear the divine verdict which condemns them to death, all of them! In a *qal waḥomer* argument, from the divine Sonship of all the Israelites, Jesus arrives at the conclusion of his own Sonship and divine dignity.

In Jn 2:17 (the zeal of Jesus), reference is made to Psalm 68:10. The context is that of the Cleansing of the Temple with a first conflict with the Jewish authorities. In Jn 12:16, there is an allusion to Psalm 118:25 (LXX 117:25). Here, more than before, we find ourselves close to the

Passion of Jesus (the Triumphal Entry). In Jn 12:38, there occurs for the first time the formula 'that the word might be fulfilled'. As C. A. Evans has shown,[13] this formula occurs in the Fourth Gospel only in the context of the Passion and beginning with the verse in question. In Jn 12:38, the unbelief of the Jews in their encounters with Jesus is explained by reference to Is 53:1 LXX. Subsequently, various aspects of the Passion of Jesus are explained with recourse to the Psalms. In Jn 13:18, the supper of Jesus with his betrayer is interpreted by using Ps 41:10. In Jn 19:24, the parting of Jesus' garments is explained by means of Ps 21:19 LXX. We must also recall the allusions to verses of the Psalms in the account of the Farewell Discourses of Jesus and of the Passion: 'they hated me without a cause' in Jn 15:25 – referring to Ps 34:19 LXX or 68:5 LXX; Jesus' thirst – referring to Ps 68:22 LXX or 62:2 LXX, or even to to Ps 41:3; 'not a bone of him shall be broken' in Jn 19:36 with a possible reference to Psalm 33:21 (the Righteous Sufferer).

The fourth evangelist is not the only one, however, to refer to what the Psalms say in his account of the Passion of Jesus: he shares in a tradition common to all the evangelists who want to make the Lord's Passion understood in the context of Scripture in general and of Israel's prayer book in particular, in other words, in the context of the Book of Psalms. It is here in particular that one comes across the figure of the Righteous Sufferer with whom Jesus is identified in his suffering. In this way, the use of the Psalms performs an apologetic aim: if non-believers wonder how it could ever be possible that the Messiah of Israel and Son of God should suffer in this way and die such a shameful death, the first Christians could have responded with a reference to the Bible in general and to the Book of Psalms in particular. If God had foreseen the suffering of Christ and foretold it, this suffering could not have happened against his will but rather have fully corresponded to his will. This view does not exclude the possibility that the fourth evangelist went beyond this apologetic vision and that he had also looked for a deeper meaning to the suffering of Jesus (cf Jn 19:36f).

---

[13] 'On the Quotation Formulas in the Fourth Gospel,' *BZ* 26 (1982) 79-83.

2. *Psalm 42/3*

Bibliography

J. BEUTLER, 'Psalm 42/43 im Johannesevangelium', *NTS* 25 (1978/79) 33-57 = ID., Studien, 77-106; ID., *Habt keine Angst. Die erste johanneische Abschiedsrede (Joh 14)* (SBS 116), Stuttgart: Katholisches Bibelwerk 1984; E. D. FREED, 'Psalm 42/43 in John's Gospel', *NTS* 29 (1983) 62-73.

Psalm 42/3 in the Synoptic Tradition

Psalm 42/3, which, according to the students of the Old Testament, forms a unity of three strophes, is utilised by the Synoptics in the account of Jesus' prayer in the Garden of Gethsemane (Mk 14:32-42 par. Mt 26:36-46, diff. Lk 22:40-46). At the beginning of his prayer, Jesus says to his disciples: 'Περίλυπός ἐστιν ἡ ψυχή μου ἕως θανάτου'. The use of the adjective περίλυπος with the substantive ψυχή is explained by scholars as a reference to Psalm 42/3 where we find in a refrain or antiphon: ῞ἵνα τί περίλυπος εἶ ψυχή (Ps 41:6, 12; 42:5 LXX). In this tradition, the Psalm is understood as a song of the 'Righteous Sufferer' and put on the mouth of Jesus in his agony.

Ps 42/3 in the account of the death and raising of Lazarus (Jn 11:1-44) and in other Johannine texts near to the Passion (12:27; 13:21):

It seems that John also used this tradition in the account of the death and raising of Lazarus. In Jn 11:32-38, the encounter between Jesus and Mary, sister of the by now dead Lazarus, is described together with Jesus' journey to the tomb. Jesus' violent emotion is described in words that are not part of the usual vocabulary of the fourth evangelist and which have aroused discussion from the time of the Fathers of the Church. In v 33, we read: ἐνεβριμήσατο τῷ πνεύματι καὶ ἐτάραξεν ἑαυτόν; the first verb expresses rage; the second is unique in the New Testament and could be derived from Ps 41:7 LXX where we find: πρὸς ἐμαυτὸν ἡ ψυχή μου ἐταράχθη. If John knew Ps 42/3 (41/2 LXX) from the Gethsemane tradition, he could have also used it freely in this account. In Jn 12:27, we find a verse which, in a sense, takes the place of the Gethsemane account in the Synoptics. Here Jesus says: Νῦν ἡ ψυχή μου τετάρακται. Some scholars refer to Ps 6:4f for these words of Jesus, also because of the following σῶσόν με (cf Nestle-Aland, Freed); however, influence from Ps 41:6, 12; 42:5 LXX and 41:7 LXX is also possible. The same goes for Jn 13:21.

Ps 42/3 in Jn 14:1-14 (and 19:28):

The beginning of Chapter 14 poses a series of problems: beside the use of the verb ταράσσεσθαι, two further elements require explanation – the exhortation to believe in God (unique in the Fourth Gospel, the only exception being Jn 5:24 which has πιστεύειν with Dative) and the use of the verb πιστεύειν in the sense of 'to have trust'. One explanation could be the evangelist's recourse to Psalm 42/3. In the 'refrain' which we mentioned previously (Ps 41:6, 12; 42:5 LXX) as in Ps 41:7, the verb ταράσσεσθαι occurs. The same 'refrain' continues: 'ἔλπισον ἐπὶ τὸν θεόν'. John would then have only replaced the verb ἐλπίζειν, foreign to his vocabulary, with his usual πιστεύειν which in this case, however, is directed also, and first, to God, and has in itself the connotation of trust. Other themes of the double Psalm occur in the section which contains Jn 14, themes such as the 'dwelling places' of God (Jn 14:2, 23; Ps 42:3 LXX); the theme of the 'way' (Jn 14:6; Ps 42:3 LXX); and that of 'truth' (Jn 14:6; Ps 42:3 LXX). It seems as if John has made use of this Psalm, which was known as a prayer of the Righteous Sufferer and had been applied to Christ, and that he interpreted it in its other dimension, that is as the prayer of a pilgrim far from the Sanctuary of Jerusalem who expresses his nostalgia for that Sanctuary. If this interpretation is correct, we could also cite Ps 41:3 ἐδίψησεν ἡ ψυχή μου πρὸς τὸν θεὸν τὸν ζῶντα (Ps 41:3 LXX) as a possible source for the words of the dying Jesus in Jn 19:28: διψῶ.

Lecture IX

Abraham

Bibliography:

H. LONA, *Abraham in Johannes 8. Ein Beitrag zur Methodenfrage* (EHS.T 65), Frankfurt/M. 1976; S. PEDERSEN, 'Anti-Judaism in John's Gospel: John 8', *New Readings in John. Literary and Theological Perspectives. Essays from the Scandinavian Conference on the Fourth Gospel Orhus 1997*, ed by J. NISSEN and S. PETERSEN (JSNT.S 182), Sheffield 1999, 172-193; H. HOET, '"Abraham is our father" (John 8:39): The gospel of John and Jewish-Christian dialogue', in: *Anti-Judaism and the fourth gospel. Papers of the Leuven Colloquium*, 2000, ed. R. BIERINGER – D. POLLEFEYT – F. VANDECASTEELE -VANNEUVILLE (Jewish and Christian heritage series 1), Assen: Van Gorcum 2001, 187-201; M. THEOBALD, 'Abraham – (Isaak) – Jakob. Israels Väter im Johannesevangelium,' in: *Israel und seine Heilstraditionen im Johannesevangelium. Festgabe für Johannes Beutler SJ zum 70.* Geburtstag, hg. von M. Labahn – K. Scholtissek – A. Strotmann, Paderborn etc.: Schöningh 2004, 158-183.

1. 'The Fathers' in John's Gospel

Having covered the role of the Scripture of Israel in John's Gospel, we can now direct our attention to the central characters of the history of Israel, and, to begin with, the Patriarchs, Abraham, Isaac and Jacob.

The passages concerning Abraham are found in the section Jn 8:31-59 which will be treated in the following at section 2.

Isaac is not mentioned in the Fourth Gospel. However, authors like M. Theobald have referred to Jn 8:56: Ἀβραὰμ ὁ πατὴρ ὑμῶν ἠγαλλιάσατο ἵνα εἴδῃ τὴν ἡμέραν τὴν ἐμήν. The name Isaac is held to derive from a Hebrew verb meaning 'to laugh': Abraham 'laughed' at the announcement of the birth of a son. According to the Christian tradition of John, the announcement of the birth of a son to Abraham finds its fulfilment in the birth of Jesus.

Two passages of John's Gospel refer to Jacob. At the end of Chapter 1, Jesus announces to his audience: 'You will see the heaven opened and the angels of God ascending and descending on the Son of Man' (1:51). This picture of the angels ascending and descending is inferred from the vision of Jacob which is described in Gen 28:12. In the original text, the angels are ascending and descending on the ladder. The text of John uses the expression 'on Him', the 'Son of Man'; inasmuch as Jesus is the person on whom the angels are ascending and descending, the experience is like that of Jacob. However, the text does not compare Jesus and Jacob directly. The *tertium comparationis* are the angels who are ascending and descending, not the person upon whom they ascend and descend. Thus Jesus appears, not as a 'new Jacob', but only as he on whom the angels ascend and descend as once they did on Jacob (M. Theobald).

The other passage that speaks of Jacob is in Chapter 9. During his journeys, Jesus crosses Samaria. In this region, he comes across a field which Jacob had given to his son, Joseph (4:5). Here was also the well named after Jacob (4:6). In what follows, this well is the object of a discussion between Jesus and the Samaritan Woman. Jesus promises the woman a water which will never fail but which will well up to eternal life. The woman does not understand this promise but interprets it on the natural level and says: 'Are you greater than our father, Jacob, who gave us this well?' (4:12). Again, Jesus does not become a 'new Jacob' but is only compared with Jacob.

2. *Abraham in Jn 8:31-59*

Abraham is cited in John's Gospel only in the section 8:31-59 where his name recurs eleven times (vv 33, 37, 39 3x, 40, 52, 53, 56, 57, 58). The starting point is a dispute between Jesus and the 'Pharisees' (8:13) or the 'Jews' (8:22) over his nature. In 8:26ff, Jesus speaks of his Father whom the Jews do not know. Jesus has been sent by the Father, and the Father does not leave him on his own because Jesus does what pleases the Father.

In 8:30, the evangelist recounts the favourable reaction of a good many of those who heard Jesus: 'At these words, many believed in him'. This is not the first time that such a favourable reaction towards

Jesus has been reported in John's Gospel. In 2:11, the disciples believe in Jesus after the sign at Cana. In 2:23, many believe in Jesus because of his signs. In 10:41f, the words of the Baptist about Jesus lead many to faith in him. In 4:39, many Samaritans arrive at faith because of the testimony of the Samaritan woman; in 4:41, on the other hand, because of the words of Jesus himself. In some cases mention is made of faith in Jesus at the beginning of a section (7:31). In other cases, such an observation is found after one of Jesus' signs (the raising of Lazarus) and before a new section (11:45) (cf Lona, 137). Cf also 12:11 and 12:42 (the faith of some members of the Sanhedrin).

On the basis of such passages, some exegetes detect 'Jewish Christians' in Jesus' audience of Jn 8:31-59. The fierce dispute between Jesus and his enemies would then be a controversy within the Christian community. However, such a simplification is not acceptable. On the contrary, it is a question, so it seems, of a dispute between a group of Jews – who are on the point of accepting faith in Christ although in a form that has not yet developed and is very near to Judaism – and Jesus. Recent scholars like Theobald highlight the fact that this dispute does not reflect historical debates between Jesus and his supporters or adversaries in Jerusalem during his lifetime but rather it is retrospective, written under the influence of the separation of Church and Synagogue towards the end of the first century in the region in which the Fourth Gospel was written.

In agreeing with the observations of H. Lona (235-244), we can say that it is possible to discern three parts in this section: vv 31-36, The Promise of Liberation; vv 37-47, The Ambiguous Fathers – the devil as father of 'the Jews'; vv 48-59, Jesus and Abraham. In all three parts, the argument turns towards Abraham.

A) The Promise of Liberation (vv 31-36)

The theme of 'freedom' dominates the whole section and frames it (vv 32 and 36). From the narrative point of view, the section is formed by a brief speech of Jesus, a reply by the hearers and a further reply by Jesus. Initially, Jesus promises the knowledge of (divine) truth and freedom (v 32) to those who continue in his word. To this promise, 'the Jews' reply that they are descendants of Abraham and so free; they have never been the slaves of anyone. In his turn, Jesus replies to this claim by explaining that they are slaves in so far as they are sinners. The slave does not continue in the house of the Master, only the Son, like Jesus: only through him can freedom be found. Already at this point, we notice a difference of perspective: for 'the Jews' what is important is physical descent from Abraham. However, this descent is not enough for Jesus. The true Sonship is the divine Sonship which guarantees freedom and is conferred by the Son. How does one arrive at this freedom? As far as the hearers are concerned, one arrives at it by accepting the words of Jesus (v 32); from the point of view of Jesus, one arrives there by means of his liberating action (v 36: Lona, 236).

B) The Ambiguous Fathers – the devil as father of 'the Jews' (vv 37-47)

From the narrative point of view, we can distinguish five contributions in this subsection: Jesus (37-38), 'the Jews' (39a-b), Jesus (39c-41a), 'the Jews' (41b-d), Jesus (42-47).

From the thematic point of view, we can distinguish (with Lona, 238f) three parts of the dialogue:
– The recalling of the fact that 'the Jews' have Abraham as their father (vv 37-39);
– The recalling of the fact of having God as Father (vv 40-42);
– The true father of 'the Jews' – the devil (vv 43-47).

The recalling of the fact that 'the Jews' have Abraham as their father (vv 37-39)

The descent from Abraham claimed by 'the Jews' is thrown into doubt by Jesus because they seek to kill him and do not accept his words (v 37): He speaks of what he has seen with his Father; they speak of what they have heard from their father (v 38). The sense of this statement is enigmatic and can be understood only in the context of the whole passage in which it appears that 'the Jews' are children of the devil. 'The Jews' leave open the question of the identity of the person of whom Jesus has spoken and claim once more their descent from Abraham (v 39a-b). Jesus' reply is that if they were Abraham's children, they would do what Abraham did (vv 39c-e). Up to this point, descent form Abraham does not seem to have a positive or decisive role for Jesus. He takes this theme from his enemies and utilises it rather *ad hominem*: if 'the Jews' claim to be children of Abraham, then they must act like Abraham. The relevance of descent from Abraham for salvation is neither confirmed nor denied.

The recalling of the fact of having God as Father (vv 40-42)

The mistaken and sinful action of the enemies consists in their attempt to kill Jesus, a man who has told them the truth entrusted to him by his Father. This is not what Abraham did (v 40). In trying to do this, 'the Jews' show themselves to be instead children of their father – a new hint at their descent from the devil (v 41). 'The Jews' sense in this rebuke an accusation of their adulterous origin and claim instead that they have one father, the only God (*ibid*). Jesus' reply puts into doubt this claim on the grounds that they do not love God: if in fact they loved God, they would also have loved Jesus who has been sent by God (v 42). The argument appears difficult and is best understood as an allusion to the 'chief commandment' of Deut 6:4ff to love the only God of Israel[14]. It can be seen how in this subsection the argument shifts from Abraham as father of 'the Jews' to God as their Father. This divine Sonship is counter posed to another, which appears here for the second time, that of the devil. This type of Sonship becomes the principal theme in what follows.

The true father of 'the Jews' – the devil (vv 43-47):

In this subsection, which consists solely of a speech by Jesus, the inability of 'the Jews' to understand his words is explained: this inability has its roots in their descent from the devil. This claim is developed in v 44. The activity of the devil is characterised by lying, on the one hand, and murder, on the other. The devil is a murderer from the beginning of humanity and does not live in the truth. While the devil tells lies, Jesus speaks the truth, but his hearers do not want to

---

[14] Cf. J. BEUTLER, 'Das Hauptgebot im Johannesevangelium', in: ID., *Studien zu den johanneischen Schriften* (SBAB 25), Stuttgart, Kath. Bibelwerk 1998, 107-120.

listen to him and believe in him. Again, it seems that the author's interest is shifting ever further from the fatherhood of Abraham. What counts is whether one has God for Father or the great adversary, the devil. If one is of God, comes from God, is son of God, he believes in the words of Jesus and finds himself on the side of truth; if, on the other hand, he comes from the devil, he belongs to the kingdom of lies and death.

C) Jesus and Abraham (vv 48-59)

Following narrative analysis, one can make out in this section three contributions of the enemies (vv 48, 52f and 57) and three of Jesus (vv 49-51, 54-56 and 58). At the end we find a non-verbal reaction of 'the Jews': they take up stones to throw at him (v 59).

A semantic analysis shows a great variety of themes. In the first exchange (vv 48-51), the subject is whether Jesus is possessed by a devil or Samaritan in origin, and therefore heterodox. Jesus justifies his words with a reference to his sincerity by virtue of which he is not seeking his own glory but that of God. Thus he can promise eternal life to those who listen to him. In the second exchange (vv 52-56), 'the Jews' renew their accusation that Jesus is possessed precisely because he promises eternal life although he himself is mortal just like Abraham and the prophets. Their question echoes that of the Samaritan Woman: 'Are you greater than our father, Jacob?' (4:12) – 'Are you greater than our father, Abraham?' (8:53). Abraham is dead and the prophets are dead: how can Jesus have eternal life and promise it? Jesus replies with a new reference to the fact that he does not seek his own glory but receives it from God. He knows the Father by contrast with 'the Jews' who do not know him. Abraham, the father of 'the Jews', rejoiced and was glad to see Jesus' day. This implies the pre-existence of Jesus or at least his presence in a vision to Abraham. 'The Jews' do not accept this claim: Jesus is not yet fifty years old and yet he thinks that he has seen Abraham? Jesus replies with the ultimate claim: 'Truly, truly I say to you: Before Abraham was, I am' (8:58). With this reply, therefore, Jesus refers pre-existence to himself. For 'the Jews', this claim of divine eternity is a blasphemy which merits the death by stoning which is appropriate to blasphemy (8:59).

3. *Final reflection*

The dialogue between Jesus and 'the Jews' on the sonship of Abraham shows a movement from the Sonship of the Israelites with respect to Abraham to the role of Abraham in the history of salvation. For the author of the Fourth Gospel, physical descent from Abraham has little importance. What is vital is the doing of the works of Abraham, works of righteousness and faith. The permanent and decisive role of Abraham was to see and announce Christ (perhaps here the intention is to give a more profound reading of the text concerning the announcement of a son for Abraham). In the end, Abraham serves only as the background to Christ: he was mortal but Jesus Christ enjoys immortality since he was pre-existent to Abraham in time –and before time.

Some scholars ask what is the importance of descent from Abraham for the Christian community of John. According to our text, there does not appear to be a positive role for Abrahamic descent for the Christians of the Johannine community. To the sonship of Abraham is opposed that which is from God, whether that of Jesus himself or that of those who believe in him. The role of Abraham is reduced to that of witness alongside Moses, the prophets and John the Baptist.

The passage that we have studied remains the most famous (or notorious) for the question of the 'anti-Semitism' of John. We have not dealt with this topic in the present lecture but have kept it back for lectures 21-22 of this course.

Lecture X

Moses

Bibliography:

H. SAHLIN, *Zur Typologie des Johannesevangeliums*, Uppsala: A. B. Lundequistska Bokhandeln 1950; J. J. ENZ, 'The Book of Exodus as a Literary Type for the Gospel of John', *JBL* 56 (1957) 208-215; R. H. SMITH, 'Exodus Typology in the Fourth Gospel', *JBL* 81 (1962) 329-342; T. F. GLASSON, *Moses in the Fourth Gospel* (SBT), Naperville, IL: Alec R. Allenson 1963; W. A. MEEKS, *The Prophet-King. Moses Traditions and the Johannine Christology* (NT.S 14), Leiden: Brill 1967; P. J. KASTNER, *Moses im Neuen Testament. Eine Untersuchung der Mosestraditionen in den neutestamentlichen Schriften*, Munich: Ludwig - Maximilians - Universität 1967; T. SAITO, *Die Mosevorstellungen im Neuen Testament* (EHS.T 100), Frankfurt a. M. etc. 1977; M. GAWLICK, 'Mose im Johannesevangelium', *BN* 84 (1996) 29-35; S. HARSTINE, *Moses as a character in the fourth gospel. A study of ancient reading techniques* (JSNT.S 229), Sheffield: Sheffield Academic Press 2002.

1. *Moses, type of Christ*

No character in the Old Testament has such an important role in John's Gospel as that of Moses. In his recent study, Stanley Harstine has marked out three forms of approach that have been applied to the question of the role of Moses in the Fourth Gospel (*op cit* 3-39). In a first phase, the scholars study the link of Moses with Jesus under the category of typology. Thus, according to H. Sahlin, Jesus is presented in the Fourth Gospel as a second Moses, but also as he who 'surpasses' Moses and every other character of the Old Testament. An important aspect for the parallelism between Jesus and Moses is the correspondence between the 'I am' speeches of Jesus and the themes of the Exodus. This parallelism confirms the impression that in Jesus, God is bestowing on his people a new Exodus with a new Passover and an eternal Sabbath in the New Covenant.

J. J. Enz takes his starting point from some formal observations relative to the comparison between the tradition of Moses in the Old Testament and that of Jesus in the Fourth Gospel. Two points of contact and similarity in these two traditions are the correspondence between 'seeing' and 'believing', and the importance of the divine Name. Just as Moses receives the revelation of God's name in the vision of the Burning Bush, so also Jesus manifests the name of the Father and – in this way – the Father himself. To these common traits can be added parallels between the activity of Moses and that of Jesus which confirm the typological link.

R. H. Smith limits his comparison between Moses and Jesus to the period preceding the Exodus of the Israelites from Egypt. All the signs worked by Moses before Pharaoh take place in this period. The author seeks to establish a strict connection between these signs worked by Moses and those performed by Jesus. The result, according to Harstine, is limited.

2. *Moses in the Fourth Gospel – the historical and theological approach*

Some scholars present the Moses of the Fourth Gospel under the historical and theological aspect without employing the paradigm of typology. The specific horizon of such studies is the Christology of the fourth evangelist. According to T. F. Glasson, the Fourth Gospel is addressed to readers who come from the standpoint of a particular Messianic expectation or, to be even more particular, one concerning the expectation of a new Moses who was to guide the People of God in the exodus from the land of slavery. In fact, themes which recall the desert abound in John's Gospel. To illustrate such messianic and eschatological expectations, Glasson has recourse to the writings of Judaism that are more or less contemporary, that is to say, the Targums and the Midrashim. Thus the hopes of Israel are seen in a more concrete form.

The classic work on the Moses traditions in the Fourth Gospel is the book of W. A. Meeks. The author, who presented his study as his doctoral thesis at the University of Yale, takes his point of departure from the confession of the crowd at the end of the 'sign' of the multiplication of the loaves: 'This is indeed the prophet who is to come into the world' (Jn 6:14) and from the subsequent comment of the narrator: 'Perceiving then that they were about to come and take him by force to make him king, Jesus withdrew again to the mountain by himself' (v 15). The two verses, taken together, show a close affinity between the two titles of 'king' and 'prophet'. How are we to explain this?

A first observation points out that Jn 6:14f is not the only passage in the Fourth Gospel in which there occurs such a linkage between the titles of Jesus as 'king' and/or 'prophet'. Already in Jn 1:20f, the people sent from Jerusalem seek from John the Baptist if he is the Christ or 'the prophet'. In Jn 7:37-52, after Jesus has made a solemn declaration about himself, a part of the crowd asks if he is indeed 'the prophet' (v 40). Another part thinks that Jesus is the Christ (v 41). There follows a discussion on the question whether the Messiah must come from Bethlehem and be of the seed of David (v 42). Meeks shows (32ff) that the section has a chiastic structure because at the end, the question if Jesus is 'the prophet' is repeated (v 52). In any case, the two titles are displayed together. A similar collocation is found in Jn 7:14-25 and 7:26-29.

Once again, the two titles appear together in Jesus' trial before the Romans in Jn 18:33-38a. Pilate asks Jesus if he is 'the king of the Jews'; Jesus gives a positive reply, but adds that he has come to bear witness to the truth: everyone who is of the truth, listens to his voice. These are the words of a prophet rather than of a king. Meeks (67) recalls the passage of Deuteronomy which speaks of 'the prophet like Moses'. It is said of him that the Jews will listen to him (Deut 18:15). It seems, therefore, that the Roman trial of Jesus connects the double tradition of the king and of the coming prophet. The title of 'king' is maintained during the Passion of Jesus, and it is proclaimed on the inscription over the cross (Jn 19:19); a *'titulus'* which Pilate retains despite the protests of the Jewish authorities.

A certain closeness of the two titles is seen also in some other passages of the Fourth Gospel. In Jn 1:49f, Nathaniel says to Jesus;

'Rabbi, you are the Son of God, you are the king of Israel'. Nathaniel arrives at this confession of faith because of what Jesus has told him about his personal experiences. In this sense, Jesus has shown himself to be a prophet, a man of God. In the Passion narrative, Jesus enters solemnly into Jerusalem: the crowd hails him with a verse of the Great Hallel in a messianic-eschatological sense: 'Hosanna! Blessed is he who comes in the name of the Lord, the king of Israel' (Jn 12:13 – Ps 118:25f). The reason for this confession of faith seems to be the presence of the crowd at the resurrection of Lazarus a (prophetic) sign of Jesus.

The two titles of Jesus linked in Jn 6:14f find their continuation in the discourse on the 'Bread of Life' in Jn 6:22-58. In this passage, Jesus is compared to Moses who gave the children of Israel bread from heaven, the manna. Jesus, by virtue of his union with the Father, gives to those who believe in him a bread from heaven which produces eternal life (not simply the sustenance for a day!). According to Meeks, John has placed this traditional account of the multiplication of the loaves in the context of the manna from heaven received by the desert generation, and has connected it with the eschatological interpretation of the unleavened bread of the Passover. Throughout the chapter it appears that the 'prophet-king' mentioned in Jn 6:14f is linked with the tradition of the 'prophet like Moses' of Deut 18:15ff. In what follows, Meeks seeks to show how the traditions about Moses offer the basis for such a vision.

In the Judaism of the period in which the Gospel was written, Philo of Alexandria is an important witness for the binomial 'priest-king'. Among the writings of the Alexandrine author, his brief work 'De vita Moisis' is the most important for our purpose. This text of Philo serves an apologetic aim. Philo wants to show his readers, non-Jews of Hellenistic culture, that Moses, the 'founder' of the Israelite religion, corresponds to the ideals of Hellenistic society. For Philo, Moses is at one and the same time king, prophet and priest. He is the king who corresponds to the Hellenistic ideal of the just king; but he is also a prophet, a description which does not have a straightforward parallel in Greek culture. In so far, however, as he could be called ἱεροφάντης, Moses corresponds to the description of 'seer' who can pronounce sacred 'oracles' for the people. Finally, Moses is also priest, a dignity normally shared with the king in antiquity. In all this, Moses shows himself in every respect equal, if not superior, to the kings of antiquity.

The most famous contemporary of Philo is Josephus. Born and brought up in the Holy Land, he was of Palestinian origin. It was there that he joined in with the revolt against the Romans before crossing over to the enemy as prisoner and then as historian. In his works one notes, like in Philo, his closeness to the proto-Rabbinic traditions. According to Josephus, Moses is the lawgiver who proclaims to the people the laws revealed to him by God himself. He appears as στρατηγός, military commander, and as ruler of the people. By contrast with Philo, for Josephus, Moses is not a king. He is not even High Priest, though he exercises sacerdotal functions. He can be called, therefore, a prophet in the full sense, even '*the* prophet' (cf Meeks, 131-146). In comparing the passages quoted, one can say that the figure of Jesus as the 'new Moses' in John finds more parallels in Philo than in Josephus.

The tradition of Moses as prophet-king is also found in the pseudepigraphical Jewish literature. Meeks (147ff) refers, among other things, to a passage of Pseudo-Ezekiel in which Moses has a vision which is interpreted subsequently by his father-in-law: Moses sees himself enthroned by God and he is promised the ability to see not only the present but also the past and the future. In other apocryphal and pseudepigraphical texts, Moses appears as either king or prophet.

The Qumran community looked forward at one and the same time to the Messiah of Aaron (priestly) and of Israel (royal), and 'the prophet', or 'a prophet' as is evident from 1QS 9,11 (Meeks, 168). The title of 'king' is denied to the Messiah because it does not conform to the ancient traditions of Israel and has been compromised by now in the time of the Hasmoneans (the historical period in which the rulers of Israel had illegally connected the royal dignity with the one of the High Priest). The same expectation of a 'prophet like Moses' in the sense of Deut 18:15ff is attested in a document from the fourth cave at Qumran: 4QTest. Here, Deut 5:28-29 and 18:15-18 are linked with Deut 33:8-11, a passage which refers to the Messiah of Aaron, and Num 24:15-17, a text which refers to the Davidic Messiah (symbolised by a star, Meeks 169). Thus 'the prophet' of Deut 18:15-18 is interpreted as an eschatological figure with a dignity comparable to that of the two Messiahs, of Aaron and Israel. However, in the Qumran documents, Moses himself is never seen as king or priest. The eschatological prophet will be like him, but clearly distinct from the Messiahs of Aaron and Israel, and indeed from priests of any variety.

In the Rabbinic tradition, Moses is seen as the prophet *par excellence*. More rarely is he described as king. The basis for this title is Deut 33:5 (Meeks, 196). Moses is the great lawgiver who has transmitted the divine legislation of the Torah to his people. In the end, he leaves to his successor, Joshua, the responsibility for the people and for the law. According to a Jewish tradition, Moses ascended from Sinai to heaven, in the presence of God, where he was enthroned as King of Israel and from where he returned to announce the divine law, the Torah, to the people, as the basis of this rule. In the Samaritan texts, Moses is called 'prophet' but not 'king'. In the Mandean texts, both titles for the revealer are lacking.

How was the Jewish tradition about Moses used in the Fourth Gospel? We have already spoken about the role of the Scripture and of the Torah of Moses in the fourth and fifth lectures. For other aspects, John emphasises at the same time both the correspondence between Jesus and Moses and the difference between the two. The Torah was given to the people through the mediation of Moses, but not by Moses himself. Jesus announces the words which God himself has revealed to him and he speaks in the name of God. The key text in this connection is Jn 1:17: 'The law was given by Moses, grace and truth came through Jesus Christ'. Contemporary authors prefer to regard this parallelism not as antithetical but as synthetic: the revelation which comes in Jesus goes beyond that given through Moses.

Moses did not give the fathers bread from heaven whereas God (in Jesus) gives the true bread to the Israelites and to whoever believes in Jesus.

Moses erected the serpent in the wilderness to protect the people. Jesus will himself be raised up on the cross to give eternal life to all who believe (Jn 3:14f).

Just as Moses ascended to heaven, so also the Son of Man will ascend to heaven to be exalted and glorified. It can be seen that in all three cases, there is an analogy between Moses and Jesus – equality in diversity – but also an advance, in Jesus, in the crossing from the reality of the Old Testament to that of the New.

3. *Moses in the Fourth Gospel – the literary approach*

Let us return briefly to Harstine, the author quoted above (cf p 65): he himself proposes a literary approach to the figure of Moses in the Fourth Gospel. In the footsteps of his master, R. A. Culpepper, he analyses the Fourth Gospel with the methods of narrative analysis. In the first chapter, he analyses the character of Moses in John's Gospel. Three functions of Moses come into focus: he is the historical anchor of Jesus, the witness and the point of conflict (cf Harstine, 161).

In the Synoptic Gospels, Moses is presented as the historical anchor of Jesus, the point of conflict, the witness and the synonym for the Torah. In the Jewish narrative tradition of the Second Temple, Moses has four functions (*ibid*):
  – to authorise the Law
  – to authenticate religious practice
  – to serve as example of piety
  – to be the prophet *par excellence*
Among themselves, these texts show great differences.

In the end, Harstine compares the figure of Moses with that of Homer in Hellenistic culture. In the Hellenistic texts, Homer has three functions: to give the author the opportunity for a quotation, to serve as an authority in various areas of knowledge and to act as expert witness.

Once again, we see some elements that are shared with the tradition of Moses in the Fourth Gospel. It is evident that the literary contacts with the Jewish tradition are the strongest.

Lecture XI

The Servant

Bibliography:

W. THÜSING, *Die Erhöhung und Verherrlichung Jesu im Johannes-evangelium* (NTA 21,1), Münster: Aschendorff 1960; C. A. EVANS, 'Obduracy and the Lord's Servant', in: ID. (ed.), *Early Jewish and Christian Exegesis. FS W. H. Brownlee* (Scholars Press. Homage Series), Atlanta: Scholars Press 1987, 221-236; G. DAUTZENBERG, 'ἀμνός κτλ', *EDNT* I (1990) 70-72; J. BEUTLER, 'Lamm Gottes', *LThK³* 7 (1997) 623s.; ID., 'Greeks come to see Jesus (John 12,20f.)', *Bib.* 71 (1990) 333-347 = ID., 'Griechen kommen, um Jesus zu sehen (Joh 12,20f.)', in: ID., *Studien zu den johanneischen Schriften* (SBAB 25), Stuttgart: Katholisches Bibelwerk 1998, 175-189.

1. *Is the 'Servant of God' in John's Gospel?*

Videtur quod non: (thus St Thomas frequently begins his questions for discussion). Indeed, the phrase 'παῖς (τοῦ) θεοῦ' never occurs in the Fourth Gospel. For this reason, bibliographies on John's Gospel omit this concept[15]. However, some bibliographical indications can be found under the phrase 'Lamb of God' in the various Biblical and theological dictionaries (cf *supra*).

Sed contra, it has to be said that the 'reality' of the Servant of God has an important role in John's Gospel. In fact, the Suffering Servant seems to form a frame for the narrative part of the Gospel before the Passion, beginning with the double description of Jesus as 'Lamb of God' by the Baptist in Jn 1:29, 36 up to Chapter 12, verses 20-43 where the theology of the Servant is dominant as we shall see below. (Cf also *supra*, sixth lecture). The figure of the Servant of God appears in the Book of Isaiah in four passages: Is 42:1-10; Is 49:1-7; Is 50:4-11; Is

---

[15] Cf. most recently that of G. VAN BELLE, *Johannine Bibliography 1966-1985. A cumulative bibliography on the Fourth Gospel*, (CBRA 1), Leuven: Acc. Reale 1988.

52:13-53:12. We shall look at how this complex of motifs is employed in John.

2. *The influence of the Servant Songs in John's Gospel before Chapter 12*

A) The Lamb of God

The expression with which John the Baptist designates Jesus at the beginning of his public life in Jn 1:29, 36 remains somewhat obscure. In exegesis that is more traditional and historicist, and which wants to safeguard this double description by the Baptist as a historical memory, the suggestion that we see in the Greek phrase ὁ ἀμνὸς (τοῦ θεοῦ) the equivalent of the Aramaic expression טַלְיָא has become well known. This term has a double signification in Palestinian Aramaic: 'lamb' and 'servant'. According to this theory, the Baptist would have used this word deliberately in a double sense in order to apply it to Jesus.[16] However, this hypothesis seems to have been abandoned, and scholars now prefer to interpret the Johannine passage in the light of the Servant who – according to Is 53:7 – 'like a lamb that is led to the slaughter, and like a sheep that before its shearers is dumb, so he opened not his mouth'. Of the Servant it is said in conclusion: 'He bore the sin of many and made intercession for the transgressors' (53:12). That fits in well with the Johannine text.

B) The light to the nations

A second point of contact between the first part of John's Gospel and the Servant Songs is found in the expression 'the light to the nations', applied to the Servant of God. This description of the Servant is found already in the First Song (Is 42:1-10): 'I, the Lord, have called you in righteousness, I have taken you by the hand and kept you; I have given you as a covenant to the people, a light to the nations' (42:6). The same affirmation is repeated in the Second Song of Is 49:1-7, in 49:6. It does not matter whether the Servant is given an individual or a collective interpretation: whatever the case, the Servant of God will have a role of enlightening the peoples. In John's Gospel, this idea

---

[16] Cf. J. JEREMIAS, *ZNW* 34 (1935) 115-123.

returns in the claim repeated several times by Jesus: 'I am the light of the world' (Jn 8:12; 9:5; cf 1:4f; 12:35, 46).

C) The One anointed by the Divine Spirit

In the First Servant Song, God proclaims at the beginning: 'I have put my Spirit upon him, he will bring forth justice to the nations' (Is 42:1). A certain resuming of these prophetic words is found in Jn 1:32f in the scene that corresponds to that of the Baptism of Jesus in the Jordan.

D) The One who opens the eyes of the blind

A final literary contact between the Servant Songs and John's Gospel – and this list is not exhaustive – can be seen in the announcement of the First Song: '(I have called you...) to open the eyes that are blind, to bring the prisoners out of the dungeons...' (Is 42:7). Like that Servant, Jesus too opens the eyes of a blind man (Jn 9) and enlightens those who open themselves to his words with the gift of sight.

3. *The influence of the Servant Songs in Jn 12*

The chapter in which the influence of the Servant Songs, and in particular the Fourth Song (Is 52:13-53:12), is most marked is the twelfth.

A) Is 52f in Jn 12:37-43

The prophet Isaiah has a special role in Jn 12:37-43. The prophet is named a good three times (vv 38, 40 and 41). These three occurrences are connected with the structure of the passage. In v 37, the evangelist notes the unbelief of Jesus' Jewish interlocutors in their confrontations with him, despite the many miracles he has worked. A reason for this is supplied in v 38: it was foretold by the prophet Isaiah (53:1 LXX). The evangelist follows this by observing the inability of the Jews to believe in Jesus (v 39). This too was foretold by the prophet Isaiah (6:10). Finally, the evangelist replies to the question as to how on earth it was possible for Isaiah to speak of Jesus (v 41). The reply is located in the interpretation of the vision which Isaiah had on the occasion of his calling as prophet (Is 6:1-8). In this vision, Isaiah sees the glory of the Lord (v 3). This glory is interpreted by John as the glory of the pre-existent Jesus. On seeing the glory of God, the prophet sees already the glory of Jesus, and so can speak of him prophetically. In the ensuing verses, this glory of God/Christ is set over against the glory of men or glory from men (vv 42f). The Jews, and in particular the Jewish leaders, are in the situation of having to choose between the glory of God and that of men, that is, risking their expulsion from their position and from the Synagogue because of their confession of faith in Christ. This decision is paradigmatic for John's readers.[17]

For the internal cohesion of the passage, Jn 12:20-43, it is important that, at v 38, the evangelist quotes words of the prophet taken from the Fourth Servant Song: '(Lord,) who has believed our report, and to whom has the arm of the Lord been revealed?' (Is 53:1). The initial address, 'Lord', is found only in the LXX. The fact that John inserted it in his text shows, once again, that he used the Septuagint rather than the Masoretic Text in his quotations. To sum up, we can say that John makes prolific use of the Book of Isaiah in the section 12:37-43 and that he also cites a verse from the Fourth Servant Song, immediately after the section of vv 20-36 to which we now turn.

B) Isaiah in Jn 12:20-36

In this section, it is possible to distinguish a short narrative introduction (vv 20-22) and to follow a series of words of Jesus, interrupted by comments from the crowd or the evangelist (vv 23-36). The account is set in motion by the desire of some 'Greeks' to see Jesus (v 20f). This desire is referred to Jesus by some disciples with Greek names (Philip and Andrew) and gives Jesus the opportunity to pronounce on his own near end, which is connected, so it seems, with the arrival of the 'Greeks' (that is, non-Jews) at salvation.

---

[17] Cf. J. BEUTLER, 'Die Ehre Gottes und die Ehre der Menschen im Johannes-evangelium', *GuL* 76 (2003) 83-91; ID., 'Faith and Confession: The Purpose of John', in: *Word, Theology, and Community in John*, ed. J. PAINTER, al., St. Louis, Missouri: Chalice Press 2002, 19-31.

We can distinguish some subsections: Jesus' words in vv 23-28a are followed by a voice from heaven (v 28bc). This voice is interpreted first by the crowd (who seem to have heard thunder or the voice of an angel) in v 29 and then by Jesus himself in vv 30-32. Finally, the evangelist elaborates still further this interpretation given by Jesus, in v 33. The last part of the section takes the form of a verbal exchange between Jesus and his interlocutors. Jesus replies to a question of the crowd (v 34) with a final contribution (v 35f).

From the semantic point of view, we can make out in this section an axis made up of the concepts of 'being glorified ($\delta o \xi \alpha \sigma \theta \hat{\eta} \nu \alpha \iota$)' and 'being lifted up/exalted ($\dot{\upsilon} \psi \omega \theta \hat{\eta} \nu \alpha \iota$)'. In vv 23-28a, the concept of 'being glorified' is introduced. This concept forms the frame of this subsection with an introduction in v 23 and a conclusion in v 28a: 'The hour is come for the Son of man to be glorified – Father, glorify you Name!' The concept is taken up at the beginning of the second subsection. The voice from heaven declares: 'I have glorified it and I will glorify it again (v 28bc). To the differing interpretations which the crowd give to this voice, Jesus adds his own in opposition: in fact, it is a question of a divine voice which announces its own imminent glorification by means of his 'lifting up/exaltation'. In this way the other key concept of this section is introduced, that of the exaltation or lifting up of Jesus (v 32): when he is lifted up/exalted from the earth, Jesus will draw all men to himself. The evangelist interprets this announcement as an indication of Jesus' salvific death (v 33). In the third subsection, vv 34-36, the concept of 'being exalted/raised up remains on its own (v 34). The people do not understand this expression. Jesus interprets it in terms of his own imminent death (vv 35f). His hearers have to decide quickly for or against him while the light is still present among them.

The title which Jesus applies to himself in this section (as elsewhere in John's Gospel) is that of 'Son of Man'. In the first use of this title in this section, Jesus says: 'Now is come the hour for the Son of man to be glorified' (v 23), and in its last occurrence, the crowd takes up Jesus' words: 'How can you say that the Son of man must be lifted up?' (v 35). The combination of the predicates 'be glorified' and 'be lifted up' with the title 'Son of Man' deserves an explanation. The derivation of these verbs from Is 52:13 LXX seems to be taken for granted. This initial verse of the Fourth Servant Song in the LXX reading is the only verse in the Bible in which the two verbs occur together with the exception of Ps 36 (37):20 LXX where it describes the condition of the ungodly prior to their abasement: a verse little suited to Christological use!

In our opinion, the fourth evangelist has used the theology of the Servant to interpret the salvific death of Jesus. The fact that so few scholars have seen clearly this recourse to Isaiah's Servant is explained by the absence of the title 'Servant of God' in John. It seems, however, that at the end of the first century AD, the various Christological titles were already interchangeable so that the predicates of one title (Servant of God) could also be attributed to another Christological title (Son of Man). In fact, in the Synoptic tradition, the title of 'Son of Man' was linked with the tradition of the Passion, Death and Resurrection of Jesus right from the three Passion predictions in Mk 8:31 par; 9:31 par; 10:31-34 par. The fourth evangelist has connected this tradition with that of the Servant so as to be able to interpret the Passion of Jesus under the Christological aspect (Jesus 'lifted up' in the double sense of that word – on the cross and with the Father –and glorified) and the soteriological: the imminent death of Jesus will be the entry point for the salvation of the Gentiles.

C) Isaiah in Jn 12:20f

Once the connection between Jn 12:20-43 and the Book of Isaiah in general and the Fourth Servant Song in particular has been noticed, we can also explain the unexpected desire of 'the Greeks' to 'see' Jesus in John 12:20f by recourse to the Fourth Servant Song. As I have sought to show in my article 'Greeks Come to See Jesus', John seems to have used Is 52:15 LXX to introduce the theme of 'seeing' Jesus. In that verse, according to the Septuagint, the peoples will wonder at the Servant and kings will shut their mouths 'because they to whom no report was brought (concerning him) shall see, and they who have not heard shall understaand. The translator of the LXX has referred the relative pronoun אֲשֶׁר not, as in the Masoretic Text, to things never seen and heard but to the people who have never seen and heard. This understanding of the verse of the MT is possible from the linguistic point of view and would fit in well with a missionary environment such as that of the Jews in Alexandria. On his part, Paul used Is 52:15 LXX in a missionary context in Rom 15:21. The unexpected use of the verb 'to see' for the adhesion of the Greeks to Jesus and for their acceptance of salvation in Jn 12:20ff would thus be explained.

4. *Final reflection*

From the pragmatic point of view, the figure of the Servant of God has an important role for the readers of John. On the one hand, it is necessary for salvation to be given and accepted in faith. In Jn 12:20-43, and in particular in vv 37-43, faith is the dominant idea for the attitude of the hearers of Jesus and for those who observe his signs. On the other hand, faith must be confessed without fear. Whoever believes in Jesus must not fear for his social position and for the security which he enjoys in the Synagogue, but must be ready to face the consequences of his adhesion to Jesus.

In the same passage of Jn 12:20-43, there is a section which speaks expressly of the disciple's readiness to die with Jesus: Jn 12:25f. The person who 'serves' Jesus is compared to the Servant. He is to be ready to be where Jesus is and to live the same fate. In this way he will be honoured equally by the Father. The vocabulary is modified gently (διάκονος corresponds to παῖς, τιμᾶν to δοξάζειν), but the link between Jesus and his disciple is still clearly recognisable. It is not necessary to attribute these words only to a later redactor (J. Becker).

In a world in which the forces of darkness (even if they are disguised every so often as forces of light) employ all their power against those who try to serve the cause of peace and justice on the basis of their faith, the latter will find comfort in the words spoken by Jesus in Jn 12:24-26.

Lecture XII

The Spirit

Bibliography:

O. BETZ, *Der Paraklet. Fürsprecher im häretischen Spätjudentum, im Johannesevangelium und in neu gefundenen gnostischen Schriften* (AGSU II), Leiden-Cologne: Brill 1963; G. JOHNSTON, *The Spirit-Paraclete in the Gospel of John* (MSSNTS 12), Cambridge: University Press 1970; F. PORSCH, *Pneuma und Wort. Ein exegetischer Beitrag zur Pneumatologie des Johannesevangeliums* (FTS 16), Frankfurt a. M.: Knecht 1974; ID., 'παράκλητος' *EDNT* III (1993) 28f; J. KREMER, 'πνεῦμα' ibid. 117-122; I. DE LA POTTERIE, *La vérité dans Saint Jean,* I-II (AnBib 73-74), Rome: PIB 1977; S. S. SMALLEY, '"The paraclete": Pneumatology in the Johannine Gospel and Apocalypse', in: *Exploring the Gospel of John. In honor of D. Moody Smith*, ed. R. A. CULPEPPER – C. C. BLACK, Louisville: Westminster John Knox Press 1996, 289-300; T. G. BROWN, *Spirit in the Writings of John. Johannine pneumatology in social-scientific perspective* (JSNT.S 253), London: T. & T. Clark 2003.

The word πνεῦμα recurs twenty four times in John's Gospel. We shall leave out the two occurrences in which it signifies the spirit or the soul/mind of Jesus (Jn 11:33; 13:21 – cf *supra*, VIII Lecture). The remaining occurrences can be assigned to three different contexts: the Spirit given to Jesus; the Spirit given by God/Jesus to the faithful; the Spirit-Paraclete given by God/Jesus to the community.

1. *The Spirit given to Jesus*

In the Fourth Gospel, as in the Synoptics, the life of Jesus begins with an account of the activity of John the Baptist. The Baptism of Jesus is missing in John's Gospel together with the opening of heaven and the voice from heaven. John is not the Baptist, as far as Jesus is concerned, but his witness (cf the inclusion between Jn 1:19 and 1:34). A divine voice addressed to John corresponds to the divine voice addressed to Jesus in the Synoptic accounts of his Baptism. John's reveals that the one on whom the Baptist sees the Spirit descend in the form of a dove will be the one who will baptize with the Holy Spirit (Jn 1:33). As F. Porsch has rightly shown,[18] behind this scene lies the First Servant Song which begins thus: Ιακωβ ὁ παῖς μου ἀντιλήμψομαι αὐτοῦ Ισραηλ ὁ ἐκλεκτός μου προσεδέξατο αὐτὸν ἡ ψυχή μου ἔδωκα τὸ πνεῦμά μου ἐπ᾽ αὐτόν κρίσιν τοῖς ἔθνεσιν ἐξοίσει (Is 42:1 LXX). The double name 'Jacob' and 'Israel' is added to the Hebrew text to ensure a collective understanding of the Song despite its not being in the original. This Song with its beginning seems to have already exercised an influence on the Synoptic tradition of the Baptism. In the Synoptics, the predicate 'he in whom my soul delights' constitutes part of the voice from heaven. This element is absent in John. Another element of Is 42:1 LXX, however, could be found in the Fourth Gospel: according to some ancient manuscripts, the reading in Jn 1:34 is: ὁ ἐκλεκτός instead of ὁ υἱὸς τοῦ θεοῦ. Undoubtedly, the gift of the Spirit to the Servant is taken up in both the Synoptics and John. This is the only element that John has taken from the Synoptics to describe the scene at the Jordan. The fact that the Spirit 'remained' on Jesus, a fact which is particular to John, seems to come from Is 11:2, a messianic text from the later layers of the Book of Isaiah (cf also Is 61:1; *PsSol* 17:37; *1 En* 49:3; 1 QSb 5:24f). The relationship between the beginning of Jesus' activity and the Servant Songs is strengthened by the double occurrence of the predicate ὁ ἀμνὸς τοῦ θεοῦ, a reference to Is 53:7, as has already been seen (cf *supra* Lecture XI). John would have, therefore, combined traditions regarding the Servant with others which derive from the conceptual world of the Messiah. For baptism with the Holy Spirit performed by Jesus according to Jn 1:33, see below, section 2.

2. *The Spirit given by God/Jesus to the faithful*

With the baptism by Jesus 'with the Holy Spirit', we arrive already at the second theme, that of the Spirit as gift of Jesus to his faithful ones. For the baptism of the faithful with a baptism with the Holy Spirit (Jn 1:33), exact parallels are absent. Porsch (*op cit,* 50) lists the 'classic' texts for the gift of the Spirit in the eschatological age: Is

---

[18] *Pneuma und Wort* 19-51.

32:15ff; 44:3ff; Ezek 36:25-29; Joel 3:1f; *TestJud* 24:2f; *PsSol* 17:29-42; 1QS 4:19-22. For the last text here, see below, section 3.

The idea of Christian baptism has its place in Jn 3:(3), 5. In his dialogue with Nicodemus, Jesus declares that it is necessary to be born 'again' or 'from above' (ἄνωθεν) in order to enter the Kingdom of God. In the following material, this declaration is explained by the need to be born again 'with water and the Spirit'. Biblical parallels for such an idea are lacking. The Old Testament knows of a divine birth of the king: Ps 2:7; 89:27, probably in a metaphorical sense in connection with his accession to the throne. A rebirth of the faithful is unknown (though cf Ps 51:12f). For the eschatological outpouring of the Spirit, one can cite the texts listed in the preceding paragraph. The Qumran community knows of the belonging of its members to the kingdom of the Spirit of truth or to that of the spirit of injustice (1QS 3:13-4:26), but without a rebirth (cf below, section 3). In the *Book of Jubilees* (1:23-25), we find the gift of the Spirit and of divine sonship to the faithful. It is only in the Gnostic texts that the concept of rebirth is fully developed: cf the treaty *De Regeneratione* (XIII) of the Corpus Hermeticum. Further details may be found in Porsch, *Pneuma*, pp 82-135.

By contrast, the following text (Jn 4:23f) links the gift of the Spirit to the eschatological age more clearly. In the dialogue with the Samaritan Woman, Jesus announces a future time, one that is imminent, in which true worshippers will worship God no longer on this mountain or that, but will worship the Father 'in Spirit and in truth'. According to Porsch, the combination of the two terms is important. God will be present in the eschatological age as the one who reveals himself in his word of truth. This point of view will find its support in the words about the Paraclete. Again, there are no antecedents for this in the canonical texts of the Old Testament, and again, it is 1QS 3:13-4:26 that offers the only convincing parallel; but the reference to God as Spirit does not find a parallel even at Qumran. Philo would be nearer to this idea.

In Jn 6:63 the Spirit, the life and the words of Jesus are brought together. The perspective is more Johannine than Biblical. We could think of the breath of life which God blew into Adam (Gen 2:7) or of God's command to Ezekiel to prophesy over the dry bones the coming of his Spirit upon them (Ezek 37:9f). The opposition between the 'flesh' that profits nothing and the Spirit which gives life is more Pauline than Biblical.

In Jn 7:37-39, there appears, more clearly than elsewhere, the connection between the gift of the Spirit and the 'hour' of the glorification of Jesus. Once again, it is appropriate to recall the passages in the Exilic and post-Exilic prophets which concern the New Covenant (cf *supra*: Jer 31:31-34 and Ezek 36:26f). The question as to whether the rivers of living water well up from the believer or rather from Jesus has still not been settled. An increasing number of scholars think of Jesus as the spring of living water. Even the text to which Jesus refers in this instance has not been established with any certainty, but a good possibility would be Psalm 78:16.[19] In any case, an allusion to the rock from which water came forth during the journey of the children of Isarel across the desert seems probable. In this case, Jesus would be being compared to that rock, as happens also in 1 Cor 10:4. It is not necessary to suppose here a literary dependence of John on Paul. It is sufficient to reckon on a common (Christian) midrashic tradition.

3. *The Spirit-Paraclete given by God/Jesus to the community*

The historical and linguistic background to the Johannine Paraclete has been studied by O. Betz[20]. Summarising his studies, he observes that heavenly personages which intercede for people under accusation exist in Second Temple Judaism and are presupposed also at Qumran. The texts then known from the Qumran community were *Jubilees*, *1 Enoch* and TestLev; in these, however, the title of 'Paraclete' is lacking. This absence is to be explained with reference to the Hebrew judicial system which knows only various types of 'witness' and does not distinguish between witnesses for the prosecution and witnesses of the defence. In the Rabbinic texts, these latter are called 's‿negor' or 'p‿raklita', with words borrowed form the Greek.[21] Heavenly

---

[19] Cf. Boismard, quoted by Porsch, *op. cit.*, 59.

[20] *Op cit.*

[21] Betz, 138.

personages who intercede for the afflicted people of God are found in the literature of the period: Noah, Enoch, Moses and Elijah. They are distinguished from the Johannine Paraclete by the fact that they are men who have gone up to heaven and not heavenly messengers.[22]

The introduction of the Spirit-Paraclete in Jn 14:16f.

The first promise of the Holy Spirit is contained in Jn 14:16f in connection with the vocabulary of the Covenant (cf, *supra*, Lecture V). To those who are faithful to the commands of God is promised the God's gift of his Spirit according to Ezek 36:26f (the verb δώσει renders the Hebrew נתן of this verse in Ezekiel). This Spirit will be given to the disciples at Jesus' request. He will be 'another Paraclete' who will take the place of Jesus to intercede for his followers with God (cf 1 Jn 2:1; Rom 8:34; Heb 7:25; 9:24).

In our group of verses, the Holy Spirit is called 'the Spirit of truth' for the first time. The Jewish antecedents for this expression are found in *TestJud* 20:1, 5 and in the Qumran texts. Betz thinks of Persian dualism for this idea.[23] In 1QS 3:13-4:26, the 'Spirit of truth' and that 'of injustice' (עולה) are opposed. For the 'Spirit of truth', cf in particular 1QS 3:19; 4:21, 23. These spirits are angels (cf 3:20f, where the 'Spirit of truth' is called 'Prince of truth' and his adversary 'angel of darkness', and 3:24 where the 'Spirit of truth' is called 'angel of truth'), but at the same time they are also warring inclinations/ tendencies in the heart of the faithful disciple. He must decide if he wishes to follow the Spirit of truth (revealed by God) or the spirit of injustice. In John, the Spirit of truth appears clearly as a reality that comes from outside and from on high, whether it is personal or impersonal. For the first possibility, scholars refer with justice to the fact that the Paraclete is referred to with the masculine personal pronoun in 14:26 after the appositional phrase τὸ πνεῦμα τὸ ἅγιον and that personal activities such as help and intercession are attributed to him.

---

[22] *Ibid.*, 146.
[23] *Op.cit.* 147ff.

The other elements of John 14:16f appear to be more Johannine: both the fact that the world cannot receive the Spirit and understand him, and the fact that the disciples are able to see him and receive him. That the Spirit will 'remain' among and in the faithful could come from Ezek 37:26 in the context of the New Covenant.

The function of the Sprit-Paraclete according to Jn 14:26

While in Jn 14:16f, the abiding of the Spirit in or in the midst of the faithful is described, his activity is described for the first time in 14:26. This activity, in the words about the Paraclete in John 14-16 is twofold: *ad intra* and *ad extra*. Ad intra, the activity of the Spirit-Paraclete refers to the person and words of Jesus. The Spirit will take the place of Jesus (as 'another Paraclete', cf 14:16), he will recall the words of Jesus to the disciples and he will teach them the right understanding of these words. This Spirit is given by the Father but sent 'in the name of Jesus', at Jesus' request and on his behalf. The function of the Spirit ad extra will be developed in Jn 15-16 (see below).

For the first time, in Jn 14:26, the Spirit-Paraclete is named 'the Holy Spirit'. This expression is already to be encountered in the Bible (cf Ps 51:13; Wis 1:5) and recurs repeatedly in the Qumran texts (cf 1QS 4:21; 1QSa 2:23 with allusion to Is 11; 1QH 7:6f; 12:12; 14:13; 16:2f; 17:26; 18 with reference to Jer 31:31ff).

The Spirit-Witness in John 15:26

According to various scholars – and the hypothesis is one to which I myself subscribe -, Chapters 15-17 appear as a *relecture* of a first Farewell Discourse in Jn 14 in the course of which the role of the Spirit appears to have been gently modified. By contrast with Jn 14, the Spirit is now given by Jesus himself, something which appears already in Jn 15:26. His task is that bearing witness for Jesus in the 'grand assize' between Jesus and the world which pervades the Fourth Gospel.[24] The testimony of the disciples is added to that of the Spirit (v 27). Thus, in the 'time of the Church', the manifold testimony of the Baptist, the Father, the works of Jesus and the Scriptures to Jesus (cf Jn 5:31-40) is

---

[24] cf. J. BEUTLER, *Martyria*, Frankfurt a. M. 1972.

prolonged through the testimony of the Spirit and of the disciples. The text nearest to ours is that from *TestJud* 20:1-5 already mentioned (*supra*, section 2) for the 'Spirit of truth'.

The Spirit-Paraclete as judge in Jn 16:7-11

Once again, the Spirit appears in his function ad extra in Jn 16:7-11. The disciples will find themselves in a situation of persecution. In that moment the divine Spirit will come to their aid. He 'will convince the world of sin, of righteousness and of judgement'. The function of the Spirit is always forensic, but in this case he assumes the role of prosecutor rather than that of defender (Paraclete). As defender, he will reveal himself only indirectly because he will take the part of the persecuted disciples. The Jewish traditions which can be cited in this regard are the same as those which we have given for the concept of the Paraclete (cf, *supra*).

The Divine Spirit as guide in the teaching of Jesus according to Jn 16:12-15

One last time, the function ad intra of the Spirit towards the disciples as a group is described. He, the 'Spirit of truth' will introduce the disciples into all truth, not revealing new content but leading the disciples further in their understanding of the words of Jesus. By contrast with Jn 14:26, it is now added that the Spirit will also announce the future to the disciples. With this '*relecture*' the function of the Spirit is broadened and prolonged into the 'time of the Church'. Various authors have recently emphasised the importance of this perspective for the understanding of the Fourth Gospel.[25]

Returning to our question concerning the Jewish background of the Fourth Gospel, it is worthwhile to recall what we have said before about the connections between the various eschatological promises attested by the Exilic and post-Exilic prophets and taken up again by Jesus according to John (cf *supra*, Lecture VI). The 'key' text for the connection of these promises among themselves and with the idea of

---

[25] J. ZUMSTEIN, A. DETTWILER, J. BECKER: *ZNW* 89 (1998) 217-234; J. RAHNER: *ZNW* 91 (2000) 72-90; C. DIETZFELBINGER; K. SCHOLTISSEK; C. HOEGEN-ROHLS, *et al.*

the Kingdom of God is found in Rom 14:17: 'For the kingdom of God does not mean food and drink, but justification (better: righteousness) and peace and joy in the Holy Spirit'. As has been seen, these promises recur together in Jn 16:4b-33 and, without the theme of 'righteousness', in 14:25-29 and 20:19-23 also. The Holy Spirit, therefore, belongs to these promises, certainly on the basis of the announcement of the new Covenant in Ezek 36:26f. The Easter passage of Jn 20:19-23 proclaims that these promises have been fulfilled.

Lecture XIII

The Shepherd

Bibliography:

A. J. SIMONIS, *Die Hirten-Rede im Johannes-Evangelium. Versuch einer Analyse von Joh 10,1-18 nach Entstehung, Hintergrund und Inhalt* (AnBib 29), Rome: PIB 1967; P.-R. TRAGAN, *La parabole du "pasteur et ses explications Jean 10,1-18. La genèse, les milieux littéraires* (StAns 67), Rome: Herder 1980; J. BEUTLER, 'Der alttestamentlich-jüdische Hintergrund der Hirtenrede in Johannes 10', in: ID. - R. T. FORTNA, ed., *The Shepherd Discourse of John 10 and its Context* (MSSNTS 67), Cambridge etc.: Cambridge University Press 1991, 18-32.144-147 = ID., *Studien zu den johanneischen Schriften*, 215-232; MARY KATHERINE DEELEY, 'Ezekiel's shepherd and John's Jesus', in: *Early Christian Interpretation of the Scriptures of Israel. Investigations and Proposals*, ed. C. A. EVANS – J. SANDERS (JSNT.S 148 = *Studies in Scripture in early Judaism and Christianity*, 5), Sheffield: JSOT Press 1997, 252-264.

Among the Christological titles present in John's Gospel, that of 'Shepherd' has aroused particular attention on the part of students. In this lecture, we shall pay heed only to the diachronic studies of this theme in John. Basically, we can distinguish three more or less recent approaches. A. J. Simonis explains the metaphorical world of the 'shepherd' in Jn 10 by recourse to the historical situation of the period in which the debates between Jesus and his adversaries in Jn 10 were situated. The author assumes a date close to AD 70 for the redaction of the Fourth Gospel. The 'thieves' and 'robbers' of Jn 10 would, therefore, be the Zealots who tried to take control of the people of God. The readers must be alerted to such a possibility. In another model, the good and bad shepherds would be those found among the first Christian community. This is the approach of P.-R. Tragan OSB. This author understands the controversy of Jn 10 against the background of Jn 21:15-17: the charge given to Peter to feed or 'pasture' the Lord's sheep. The passage in Jn 10:1-8 would represent an anticipation of this charge.

The road taken by the majority of exegetes today is that which sees behind Jn 10:1-8 some texts of the Old Testament and of Second Temple Judaism which speak of the King of Israel in the past and a future king of the people (heavenly or earthly). This will be our approach.

Chapter 10 of John was the topic of a seminar of the 'Studiorum Novi Testamenti Societas' (SNTS), presided over by yours truly together with R. T. Fortna in the years 1985 and 1986. The results were published in the volume indicated in the bibliography. Among the participants in this seminar, there was agreement, on the fact that the immediate context of the Good Shepherd Discourse in Jn 10:1-8 must be sought in Jn 9.[26] It is not appropriate to regard the discourse of Jn 10 as a 'fragment without context' as was held by Bultmann and other scholars. There is no lack of an audience at the beginning of the chapter, as one might have expected, but this is easily explained if the discourse of Jn 10:1-18 is inserted into its narrative context. The discourse follows the controversies between Jesus and the Pharisees or 'the Jews' of Chapter 9. While the man born blind acquires his sight, Jesus' opponents show themselves ever more shut up in the world of darkness and, for this reason, inexorably blind. Thus the discourse is addressed precisely to the Pharisees (as representatives of a Judaism opposed to faith in Jesus) who were last mentioned in 9:40. It is they to whom Jesus addresses the parable of Jn 10:1-5: Ταύτην τὴν παροιμίαν εἶπεν αὐτοῖς ὁ Ἰησοῦς (10:6) and the ensuing discourse. It is not necessary to widen this narrative context to include Jn 8 and Jn 11 as suggested by M. K. Deeley: but it is undoubtedly evident that the author of Jn refers in 10:19-21 to the healing of the man born blind recounted in Jn 9.

---

[26] On the basis of C. H. DODD, *The Interpretation of the Fourth Gospel*, Cambridge: UP 1953.

1. *Verbal correspondence between the themes of the Good Shepherd Discourse of Jn 10 and the traditions of the Old Testament* [27]

Recent authors who have examined the Old Testament quotations in John's Gospel (E. D. Freed; G. Reim; M. J. J. Menken) have not found any explicit Old Testament quotations in Jn 10:1-18, 26-30. What has been discovered are allusions or motifs common to the Old Testament and John. According to Tragan, the correspondences are above all:

- the shepherd who guides his flock (Is 40:11)
- the Servant who consecrates himself to death (Is 53:12)
- the 'gathering' of the sheep (Is 56:8; Ezek 34:13; 37:21-22)
- the 'one' shepherd (Ezek 34:23; 37:21-24)
- the shepherd who leads the just 'in pastures green' (Ps 23:1-3)
- God as shepherd of Israel, 'the people of his pasture, the sheep of his hand' (Ps 95:7).

2. *Thematic Correspondences between the themes of the Good Shepherd Discourse of Jn 10 and the Jewish tradition* [28]

A) Evil shepherds and wolves

As shown by J. Jeremias,[29] the title of 'shepherd' was not applied to the King of Israel in pre-Exilic times. This title was used for the kings of the neighbouring countries to identify their rulers. In Israel, the title, applied to human rulers, enjoyed sparse popularity not least because of the poor reputation which shepherds had in Israelite society: they were people who were literally on the margins of society, endowed with scant social education and therefore loathed. It was only in the Exilic and post-Exilic age that the title received a good connotation.

In some texts of the Exilic age, we find the title of 'shepherd' applied to the kings and rulers of Israel in a negative sense. The prophets of this period accuse the 'shepherds' of Israel of their wicked rule over the people. In Jer 23:1-2, we find words of the prophet

---

[27] Cf. TRAGAN, *op. cit.*, 242-243; BEUTLER, *Shepherd Discourse*, 25.
[28] For this section cf. BEUTLER, *op. cit.*, 25-31.
[29] Art. 'ποιμήν', TDNT VI (1968) 485-502.

Jeremiah against the shepherds of Israel: just as already, in Jer 10:21, he has rebuked them for having neglected the flock and so of being the cause of their being scattered. In Jer 23:3-4, God announces that he himself will gather his people from all the nations, that in future he will be the shepherd of his people for whom he himself will provide new shepherds. This promise is refined in what follows with an announcement of a new Son of David. The section closes with the announcement of a new Exodus (vv 5-6).

The 'classic' text on the wicked shepherds of Israel is found in Ezek 34. The chapter has probably been redacted over a period of time. Dependence on the text of Jer 23 is not certain. In any case, the figure of the shepherd who neglects his sheep was 'in the air'. In the first ten verses, Ezek 34 begins with words of judgement on the shepherds of Israel who 'feed themselves'. The core of the 'trial' is found already in vv 1-2 and developed in vv 3-4. In vv 5-6, the consequences of the shepherds' behaviour is described: the flock is scattered and threatened by wild animals. After a recapitulation about the failings of the shepherds (vv 7-8), God pronounces his verdict on the shepherds: they will be dismissed (vv 9-10). God himself will take the place of the shepherds (vv 11-16) and – in a change of image – he will judge between sheep and sheep, between sheep and goats (vv 17-22). There follows the announcement of a new shepherd whom God will give to the people (vv 23-24, cf Jer 23) and of a New Covenant of peace between God and his people (vv 25-31).

God's words of judgement on the wicked shepherds seem to include a verdict on the ruling class of Israel as well. This appears, among other things, from some passages that make a comparison between the chiefs of Israel and ravening wolves (Ezek 22:27; Zeph 3:3).

In the later period of the Old Testament we find other passages that announce God's judgement on the shepherds of Israel (Zech 10:2f – 'sheep without a shepherd'!) The subject is taken up again in the pseudepigraphical literature of the Second Temple period, the Visions of Enoch among other texts (*1 En* 83-90). These visions date from

about the years 175-165 BC according to the estimate of M. Black.[30]
The twelve tribes of Israel are represented by the image of sheep; Egypt
appears under the figure of a wolf, Saul as a ram who wounds the sheep
entrusted to him. The rulers of the post-Exilic period up to the time of
the Maccabees appear as wicked shepherds to whom the divine
judgement is announced. A pseudepigraphic fragment of Ezekiel,
edited by A.-M. Denis, takes up the themes of Ezek 34 with the
announcement of the judgement of the shepherds of Israel and the
separation between ram and ram, calf and calf.[31] This text dates from
the period between the Roman invasion of Palestine (63 BC) and the
time of the redaction of the *Antiquitates Judaicae* of Josephus (c AD
50). A similar text comes from the period of the redaction of the Fourth
Gospel: we find it in the *Fourth Book of Ezra* in which Ezra prays God
not to abandon the flock whom he has gathered (8:29). In the same
book, Fealtiel, prince of the people, prays Ezra not to abandon the
people like a shepherd who leaves his sheep to the ravening wolves
(5:18). In a literal, not metaphorical sense, *TestGad* 1:2-4 speaks of the
defence of the people from lions, wolves and other wild animals.

B) The eschatological good shepherd

A large number of texts speak of a future shepherd of Israel.[32] Of
those from the pre-Exilic period, we do well to recall Gen 48:18; 49:24;
Hos 4:16; Pss 28:9; 80:2 and possibly 23:1-3. From Exilic or Post-
Exilic times should be mentioned Pss 74:1; 77:21; 78:52; 79:13; 95:7
and 100:3.

Of particular interest for our subject are the prophetic texts of the
Exilic period which speak of God as shepherd of his people. The more
satisfactory texts listed by Willmes are Jer 13:17; 23:3 and 31:10.[33] The
most important aspect of these texts seems to be the gathering of the
scattered people on the part of the God-Shepherd. Chapter 34 of

---

[30] SVTP 1, Leiden 1985.
[31] PVTG 3, Leiden 1970.
[32] Cf. B. WILLMES, *Die sogenannte Hirtenallegorie Ez 34* (BBET 19), Frankfurt a. M.
etc. 1984, 279-311.

[33] For 23:3, cf *supra*, A); for Ezek 34, cf this same paragraph.

Ezekiel seems to be presupposed in Zeph 3:19 as also in Mich 2:12; 4:6f. The Wisdom books speak of God as the one shepherd; as the one who guides all men in Sir 18:13.

From the time of the destruction of Jerusalem and the Temple in 586 BC, there also appears the divine promise of a future king of Israel who will save his people. This idea is found already in Mich 5:3 and repeated in Jer 3:15; 23:4. In Jer 23:5-6, this figure becomes more defined as the descendant of David; (at the same time, the title of 'shepherd' is replaced by that of 'king'). A similar process of clarification can be observed in Ezek 34:23f: the future, one shepherd will be the Servant of God, David, prince in Israel. David is mentioned again in Ezek 37:24 (where he is identified with the shepherd of Israel) after God will have brought back his people into the Land of Israel as a single flock (34:21-23).

The figure of a 'shepherd' (*mebaqqer*, from the root בקר) appears in the Damascus Document (CD 13:7ff). Here it is a question of the superior of the lay community of Damascus. According to Chaim Rabin, the title must go back to Ezek 34. His duties are described in CD 13:9: 'And he will have mercy on them as a father on his sons, and he wil bring back his scattered ones as a shepherd his flock' (cf Ezek 34:12, 16).

At the time of the redaction of the Fourth Gospel, the title of shepherd could be used in the Jewish environment of the New Testament to designate the Law or Wisdom. The Syriac *Apocalypse of Baruch* observes that the shepherds of Israel are no more but that the people have one shepherd, one light and one fountain in the Law and in Wisdom (77:13-17). It is not the time or place to develop a messianic reading because if this interpretation on the part of Christians; but for Jn 10, this Jewish tradition is still interesting.

C) The death of the shepherd and the salvation of the sheep

The idea that the Good Shepherd lays down his own life for his sheep finds no precedents in the Old Testament. Sometimes, reference is made to Is 53:12 which speaks of the death of the Servant of God for his own people and in expiation of their sins. In this text, however, it is not the Shepherd who is being spoken of but the Servant. The Servant is in fact compared with the sheep or the lamb (53:7).

The only text relevant for the idea of the shepherd who gives his life for the sheep is found in Zech 13:7: 'Awake, O sword, against my shepherd, against the man who stands next to me, says the LORD of hosts. Strike the shepherd, that the sheep may be scattered; I will turn my hand against the little ones'. This text has been used by the Synoptic Gospels. Mk 14:27 par Mt 26:31 suppose a version different from the original text of Zechariah and from the LXX, making God the subject of the action; God announces that he will strike the shepherd so that the sheep may be scattered. Jesus announces, at the same time, that he will go before his disciples into Galilee after his resurrection. It is possible that verse 13:7 in Zechariah already had a positive sense, since the death of the shepherd opens the way for a new gathering of the flock. This conclusion becomes possible when the stricken shepherd of Zech 13:7 is identified with the one who has been pierced in Zech 12:10 who begins the purification of the people by his death.

The text of Zech 13:7 has been taken up again by the Damascus Document (19:7ff). It concerns a word of judgement on the shepherds which prepares for an announcement of salvation for a part of the flock, 'the poor of the flock' (13:9). Their salvation and the destruction of the others with the sword are connected with the arrival of the Messiah of Aaron and Israel (19:10f).

Probably Zech 13:7 did not have a direct influence on the Good Shepherd Discourse of Jn 10. However, the verse is present in the Farewell Discourses, at least in their present form. At the end of Chapter 16 (16:32), we find an allusion to this verse of Zechariah: 'You will be scattered, every man to his home'. And, in the evangelist's reflection, the nearby text of Zech 12:10 seems to have been employed in the account of the opening of Jesus' side after his death (Jn 19:37): 'They shall look on him whom they have pierced'.

Lecture XIV

The Bread of Life

Bibliography:

P. BORGEN, *Bread from Heaven. An exegetical study of the concept of Manna in the Gospel of John and the writings of Philo* (NT.S 10), Leiden: Brill 1965; M. J. J. MENKEN, *Old Testament Quotations in the fourth Gospel* (Contributions to Biblical Exegesis and Theology, 15), Kampen: Kok Pharos 1996; J. BEUTLER, 'Zur Struktur von Johannes 6', in: ID., *Studien* 247-262 = 'The Structure of John 6', in: *Critical Readings of John 6*, ed. R. A. CULPEPPER (Biblical Interpretation Series, 22), Leiden-New York-Cologne 1997, 115-127; MIRA STARE, *Durch ihn leben. Die Lebensthematik in Joh 6* (NTA 49), Münster: Aschendorff 2004.

In Jn 6, Jesus is twice identified with the 'Bread of Life' (6:33, 48). These words are found as part of a series of similar expressions of Jesus. In fact, he declares himself to be 'the light of the world' (8:12; 9:5; cf 12:46), 'the gate' (10:7, 9), 'the good shepherd' (10:11, 14), 'the resurrection and the life' (11:25), 'the way, the truth and the life (14:6) and 'the (true) vine' (15:1, 5).

For our present course on 'Judaism and the Jews in the Gospel of John', what interests us above all is the Jewish background of the identification of Jesus with 'the Bread of Life'. We shall begin our analysis with some account of the Johannine context of the expression 'bread of life', so that we can then study the antecedents of this expression in the Old Testament and in Judaism.

1. *Jesus, 'Bread of Life' in John 6*

A) The place of John 6 in the Fourth Gospel, the origin and structure of the chapter

Still today, it remains somewhat problematic to place John 6 in its proper context. Without a particular indication of any journey of Jesus, he is found, at the beginning of Jn 6, in Galilee. Such a location is also assumed in 7:1. In the course of Chapter 7, the debates with 'the Jews' over the messianic prerogatives of Jesus and the miraculous cure of the paralytic in Jn 5 continue (cf Jn 7:21). Some authors, therefore, prefer to shift Chapter 6 before Chapter 5[34]. More recently, such attempts at transposition have been less accepted. It is not to be taken for granted that a modern reader knows better than an ancient one what must be the original place of a section: perhaps there were other criteria for the ancient author and reader to consider, criteria more important than logical succession in time or comprehensible movement in space. In our opinion, it seems that the chapter can be located in its position, probably inserted by the author himself after the redaction of chapters 5 and 7. Thus not only would the 'Eucharistic' section (Jn 6:51c-58) be 'redactional', as Bultmann thought,[35] but the whole of the chapter. The reasons for such hypotheses are: the difficulty of a coherent reading of Jn 5-7, the particular closeness of Jn 6 with the Synoptics (above all the 'Bread Section' of Mk 6:6b-8:26 parr) and the fact that Jesus celebrates this Passover not at Jerusalem but in Galilee and with strong Eucharistic elements. Thus Jn 6 could witness to the birth of a 'Christian Passover' in which not only was the Exodus of Israel from Egypt celebrated but also, and above all, the gift of the Eucharist to the Christian community. It cannot be ruled out, moreover, that *'relectures'* are to be found within Jn 6: from the Synoptic tradition of the miracle of the multiplication of the loaves to the discourse of Jesus himself as 'the Bread of Life', received in faith, right up to the last Eucharistic *relecture* which sees in Jesus the Bread of Life present in his faithful, in the sacrament of the Eucharist, under the species of bread and wine.

In order to discover the structure of Jn 6, it is appropriate to utilise the tools of narrative and semantic analysis. It is possible to see in this chapter a concentric structure:

1-15 scene with the disciples, mentioned by name 66-71
16-21 scene with Jesus and the disciples 60-65
discourse of Jesus
22-59

---

[34] So, among others, R. SCHNACKENBURG, *The Gospel according to St John,* translated from the German, II, London: Burns & Oates 1980.

[35] *The Gospel of John*, translated from the German, Oxford: Blackwell 1971.

The discourse of Jesus, or rather his dialogue (M. Stare speaks of 'Gespräch'), can itself be divided into six exchanges between Jesus and his interlocutors:

22-27 introduction/conclusion: Capernaum, Eucharistic elements 52-59
     29-29 the necessity of faith (as human-divine 'work') 41-51
          30-33 the bread of heaven 34-40

According to this structure, the words of Jesus 'I am the Bread of Life' of v 35 would find themselves at the centre of the discourse and of the chapter, at the beginning of the fourth exchange between Jesus and his interlocutors.

B) Jesus, Bread of Life

Between the exchange of vv 30-33 and that of vv 34-40 there is a progression. The first verses speak of the bread of heaven given by God or Moses. The Jews seek a sign from Jesus like that performed in the desert by Moses who gave them bread from heaven (with a reference to Scripture, probably Ps 78:24, see below). Jesus, in his turn, announces a bread from heaven which is the 'true bread', given, now, by the Father. In the verses 34-40, the nature of this bread is clarified. The Jews ask Jesus for the bread which he has announced, but they remain on the level of physical bread (like the Samaritan woman who seeks eternal water from Jesus: 4:15). Jesus, for his part, proclaims that he himself is 'the Bread of Life'; he who accepts him in faith will never die but have eternal life (35-40).

2. *The quotation of Jn 6:31*

In Jn 6:31, the Jews, in seeking a sign from Jesus, quote some words of Scripture in their support: ἄρτον ἐκ τοῦ οὐρανοῦ ἔδωκεν αὐτοῖς φαγεῖν. The provenance of this 'quotation' has not yet been established with certainty.[36]

The four Old Testament texts which could have been the basis of John 6:31 are Ex 16:4; Ex 16:15; Neh 9:15/2 Esd 19:15 and Ps

---

[36] The question has been treated in detail by J. M. M. MENKEN, *op. cit.*, 47-65.

78(77):24. In Ex 16:4, the verb 'give' is not attested and the subject who speaks is God. The object is in the plural. Influence on Jn 6:31 is, therefore, very improbable. The same goes for Ex 16:15: the grammatical form is that of words of Moses addressed to the Israelites. At the beginning, we find the demonstrative pronoun: οὗτος ὁ ἄρτος. All this is absent in Jn 6:31. Nehemiah 9:15 has, for its part, the form of an address: the Israelites are turning to God in prayer. Thus, as the text closest to Jn 6:31, there remains Ps 78(77):24. Compared with the Johannine text, we notice two differences: the form ἄρτον οὐρανοῦ instead of ἄρτον ἐκ τοῦ οὐρανοῦ, and the fact that in the Psalm, the subject is God and not Moses. As far as the first difference is concerned, Menken emphasises that the 'from' heaven is very close to the thought of John and that it is possible that the verse of Ps 77:26 LXX could have influenced the Johannine text. There it is said that God made a strong wind come ἐξ οὐρανοῦ which brought the quails to the Israelites. As for Moses, regarded as the author of the miracle of the gift of manna, Menken furnishes ample documentation which shows that already in Hellenistic Judaism of the first century AD (Philo) there exists a divinisation of Moses, partly on the basis of Ex 7:1: 'See, I make you as god to Pharaoh'. In the Rabbinic texts of the first three centuries, this idea is scarcely attested, perhaps because of the polemic against the Christians who believed in the divinity of Jesus. Later, there are numerous texts which justify this idea.

3. *The manna in the Old Testament: variations on the theme*

A) Manna and Sabbath

In the text of Ex 16 itself, (at least) two literary strata are to be observed: one, more original, which recounts the miracle of the gift of the manna and another which adds the element of Sabbath observance (vv 4-5, 22-30). The final redaction seems to date from the priestly layer of the Pentateuch, the original account from the Yahwistic stratum.

B) Manna and faith

Already in the account in Ex 16, the gift of manna and of the quails is connected with the theme of the murmuring of the people. The double gift from God serves to reinforce the people's faith.

In various passages of the Book of Exodus, miracles serve to create or renew the faith of the Israelites. At the beginning of the signs and miracles of the Exodus, we find two miracles designed to legitimate Moses before the people: the transformation of his rod into a serpent and the healing of the leprosy that covered his hand. The people see these two miracles, and the Book of Exodus concludes: 'And the people believed; and when they heard that the LORD had visited the people of Israel and that he had seen their affliction, they bowed their heads and worshiped' (Ex 4:31). After the passage through the Red Sea, there is added: 'And Israel saw the great work which the LORD did against the Egyptians and the people feared the LORD; and they believed in the LORD and in his servant Moses' (Ex 14:31). This text is of great relevance for the Fourth Gospel (cf, among others, Jn 14:1). According to Ex 19:9, the Israelites are to believe Moses because God has spoken to him from the cloud.

The Book of Numbers reports a fresh uprising of the people in the heart of the desert: there is no great lack of anything, but the Israelites would like to stone Moses, Aaron, Caleb and Joshua. At this point, 'the LORD said to Moses, "How long will this people despise me? And how long will they not believe in me, in spite of all the signs which I have wrought among them?"' (Num 14:11). Once again, the signs of the Exodus and of the desert have the aim of leading the people to faith. This faith includes faith in Moses, his brother and the heads of the people who have been authorised by God. On the other hand, faith is also required from Moses and Aaron: because they have not shown faith in God before the miracle of the water coming out of the rock, they are to be punished by him and will not enter the Promised Land (Num 20:12). The lack of faith of the people concerning the entry into The Holy Land is recounted in Deuteronomy (9:23).

Also in the Psalms, the gift of manna and the other miracles of the desert are linked with the theme of faith. In Ps 78, the list of the divine benefits during the period of the Exodus is placed in contrast with the lack of faith and obedience on the part of Israel: 'In spite of all this they still sinned; despite his wonders they did not believe' (Ps 78:32). In Psalm 105 the record of the divine marvels is inserted into a prayer of reflection on the history of Israel from the time of the Exodus: 'They asked, and he brought quails, and he satisfied them with the bread from heaven' (105:40). The purpose of all these marvels is the praise of the Lord and the observance of the divine precepts (105:45).

In the prayer of the people according to Neh 9:15, the arrogance of the people is opposed to the divine providence: 'You gave them bread from heaven for their hunger and brought forth water for them from the rock for their thirst'. These divine benefits stand in contrast with the lack of obedience of the Israelites, and with their forgetfulness of what God had done for them.

C) Manna and elements

A particular use of the motif of the manna is found in the Book of Wisdom. In this text, we find ourselves fully in the Hellenistic world. In the last lines of the book, the author recalls God's benefits towards his people, employing the Hellenistic theory of the four elements. God the Creator stands above these elements. For this reason, he can also reconcile the element of fire with the ice. The manna had a similar appearance to ice but it was not consumed by the fire. Thus is shown the omnipotence of the Creator (Wisd 19:21). The expression used to describe the 'bread of heaven' is, for its part, Hellenistic; the Greek text speaks of 'ambrosia', the food of the gods.

4. *The Bread of Life Discourse and the Hellenistic Homily*

In his work, 'Bread from Heaven', Peder Borgen takes his position from a haggadic tradition in the time of the redaction of the gospels and of the writings of Philo of Alexandria. This tradition is comparable to that listed above, section 3 (C). In fact, in the Exodus, God had changed the natural order. While in day to day experience bread comes from the soil and rain comes from heaven, he had made bread rain down from heaven and water to spurt out of the rock. The texts brought forward by Borgen to support his work are, among others: Ex.R. 25,2; 25,6; Philo, *Mos*. I 201-202; Mek. Ex 16,4; Petirat Moses and Philo, Mos II 267.[37]

---

[37] BORGEN, *op.cit.*, 7f.

According to Borgen, Philo and John have combined Biblical and haggadic traditions. As the basis of the argument of John, we find the method of *gezera shava*, the combination of two similar texts. In the homilies of the period in a Hellenistic environment, the preachers often used a text taken from the Torah in combination with another text. In Philo, this second text is taken from the Torah itself. In John, the prophets are preferred (cf Borgen, 38f). The primary text in Jn 6 would be that of Ex 16:4 or 16:15; the secondary text, Is 54:13 (quoted in Jn 6:45).

Moreover, in the Hellenistic homilies attested in Philo, the orators frequently divide a scriptural quotation into two parts which are developed one after the other. In the case of Jn 6, the first part of the quotation of Scripture (under the influence of haggadah) would be the text from Exodus: 'He gave them bread of heaven'; the continuation would be 'and they ate' (Jn 6:49). This would be the theme of the second part of the Bread of Life Discourse up to v 58. Bultmann's division according to theological character into 6:25-51b (non-sacramental) and 51c-58 (sacramental) would, therefore, be refuted.

The exegetical discussion has drawn much profit from the contribution of P. Borgen, even if discordant voices are not lacking. One necessary modification would be the choice of Ps 78:24 as the base of Jesus' discourse. As Menken notes, examples of homilies based on texts from other parts of Scripture than the Pentateuch are found. Thus, Borgen's proposal would remain valid even on the basis of Ps 78:24.

Lecture XV

The Messiah

Bibliography:

W. BITTNER, *Jesu Zeichen im Johannesevangelium. Die Messias-Erkenntnis im Johannesevangelium vor ihrem jüdischen Hintergrund* (WUNT, 2. Reihe 26), Tübingen: Mohr 1987; A. LINK, 'Botschaf-terinnen des Messias. Die Frauen des vierten Evangeliums im Spiegel johanneischer Redaktions- und Theologiegeschichte', in: J. HAINZ (Hg.), *Theologie im Werden. Studien zu den theologischen Konzeptionen im Neuen Testament*, Paderborn, Vienna: Schöningh 1992, 247-278; J. PAINTER, *The quest for the Messiah. The history, literature and theology of the Johannine community*, Edinburgh: Clark, 2. ed., 1993; D. RENSBERGER, 'The messiah who has come into the world. The message of the gospel of John', in: R. T. FORTNA - T. THATCHER (ed.), *Jesus in Johannine tradition*, Louisville, Ky. [etc.]: Westminster John Knox Press 2001, 15 – 23; K. SCHOLTISSEK, '"Mitten unter euch steht er, den ihr nicht kennt" (Joh 1,26). Dic Messias-Regel des Täufers als johanneische Sinnlinie - aufgezeigt am Beispiel der relecture der Jüngcrberufungen in der Begegnung zwischen Maria von Magdala und Jesus', in: *MThZ* 48 (1997) 103-121; STEGEMANN, EKKEHARD-STEGEMANN, WOLFGANG, 'König Israels, nicht König der Juden? Jesus als König im Johannesevangelium', in: STEGEMANN, EKKEHARD (Hg.), *Messias-Vorstellungen bei Juden und Christen*, Stuttgart: Kohlhammer 1993, 41-56.

The word χριστός is found in the Fourth Gospel nineteen times, out of 531 occurrences in the New Testament. These statistics are in themselves significant for they show that this word is not one of the Christological titles preferred by John. This impression is hugely reinforced when we study the use of this title in the Fourth Gospel.

1. *The Jewish Messiah*

Of the nineteen occurrences of the word χριστός in John's Gospel, twelve speak of the Messiah of the Jews without a particularly

Christian connotation. Often the word is found on the lips of the Jews, in other cases on the lips of John the Baptist.

When John the Baptist begins his activity beside the river Jordan, he quickly stirs up consternation among the Jewish authorities in Jerusalem. So they send him a delegation to interrogate him about his identity. The Baptist begins his reply with a negative confession: he is not the Messiah. Following this, he denies also two alternatives: that he is Elijah (*redivivus*) or 'the Prophet' (Jn 1:19-21). It can be seen from this that the title of 'Messiah' is a known quantity. Together with the title of Elijah (*redivivus*) and 'the prophet', the Baptist denies that he is one of the eschatological figures expected by the Jews as deliverer in the last times. The same titles are repeated in Jn 1:25 when the Jerusalem delegation wants to know positively who the Baptist is. Now the Baptist announces one 'who is to come' the strap of whose sandals he himself is not worthy to unloose (1:27). Another declaration of the Baptist in which he claims not to be the Messiah is found in Jn 3:28.

The debates about the person of Jesus in Chapter 7 of John are focused in part on the question as to whether Jesus is the Messiah. The question is handled above all in the debates of 'the Jews' among themselves and is not addressed directly to Jesus. In 7:26, a section of the Jerusalemites ask one another if, perhaps, the rulers of the people have recognised that he is the Messiah. In the next verse, however, this reasoning is refuted because it is known where Jesus comes from whereas this will not be true of the Messiah. Probably this is one of the examples of 'Johannine irony' because, in reality, for the readers, Jesus' origin is, at the same time, known and unknown.[38] He comes from God, and this fact is accessible only to faith. The theme of Jesus' origin is taken up again in 7:41-42. Again, the fourth evangelist recounts a debate among the Jews of Jerusalem. Some maintain that Jesus is the Messiah; others instead reply that this is not possible because the Messiah has to be descended from the dynasty of David and be born in Bethlehem. Jesus comes, however, from Galilee. Again, it is possible that here we have Johannine irony if we suppose that the

---

[38] Cf. SCHOLTISSEK, *loc. cit.*, 110.

readers of the Fourth Gospel were aware of the Synoptic tradition concerning Jesus' birth in Bethlehem.

A new element appears in Jn 7:31, still in the debates of the Jews of Jerusalem among themselves. Some of them arrive at faith in Jesus because of the signs which he does, saying: 'When the Christ appears, will he do more signs than this man has done?' The argument is not immediately convincing because miracles are not expected of the Messiah. The only branch of Judaism which connects miracles to the Messiah is that which sees in the messiah another Moses who will free the people of God from their slavery. The Rabbis know the principle: 'Just as the first redeemer, so will be the second'. Just as Moses liberated the people of God with signs and wonders, so the messiah will do in the eschatological time. We have met with his tradition in the lecture on Moses, the prophet-king (see above, lecture X).

Once again, still in the Jewish perspective, Jesus is supposed to be the Messiah in Jn 9:22. The parents of the man born blind who has been cured are frightened to confess that their son was healed by Jesus: 'for the Jews had already agreed that if any one should confess him to be Christ, he was to be put out of the synagogue'.

The next text is in Jn 10 in a scene which corresponds in part to the Jewish trial of Jesus in the Synoptics. The setting is the Feast of Dedication of the Temple. In the Temple itself, Jesus is seen sur-rounded by 'the Jews' and subjected to interrogation: 'How long will you keep us in suspense? If you are the Christ, tell us plainly' (10:24). The question corresponds to that directed to Jesus – by the High Priest according to Mk 14:61 par. It is worth comparing the two texts precisely. In Mark, the High Priest asks: 'Are you the Christ, the Son of the Blessed?' In this form, the question seems already to presuppose the Christology of the first community, and we shall see how John too develops Jesus' title as Messiah in the direction of the divine Sonship of Jesus.

One last time, Jesus is spoken of as Messiah from the Jewish point of view in Jn 12:34. In this text, we find the last dispute between Jesus and his Jewish interlocutors in Jerusalem. The question is put: how can the fact that Jesus is going away (in the hour of his exaltation) be reconciled with his being the Messiah of whom it is known that he will remain for ever. Once more, for the Christian reader, the paradox is resolved because he knows very well that the Messiah will enter into eternal life and return to be amongst his own precisely by means of his exaltation and glorification.

2. *The Samaritan Messiah*

Up to now, we have seen that none of the Jews has arrived at faith in Jesus as Messiah. The only passage that talks of an opening towards such a faith is Jn 7:31 (see above). In Chapter 4, the evangelist gives us an example of the profession of such a faith, at least in the form of a question (Jn 4:29). The Samaritan woman had encountered Jesus at Jacob's Well and had initiated a conversation with him. Jesus had revealed himself to the woman as someone who could give her living water, in a deep sense. In the ensuing material, Jesus had revealed to the woman that he knew her most personal secrets. It was then that she arrived at the conclusion that he must be a prophet (4:19). After a further revelation by Jesus concerning future worship, she says to him: 'I know that Messiah is coming (he who is called "Christ")' (4:25). Jesus replies to her: 'I who speak to you am he' (v 26). This self-revelation is accepted by the woman who says to her fellow-citizens: 'Come, see a man who told me all that I ever did. Can this be the Christ?' (v 29).

Scholars emphasise three aspects of this passage:
– the identity of the Samaritan Messiah as he 'who is to come' (aram. *Taheb*)
– the first profession of faith in Jesus as Messiah as something which happens in Samaritan territory
– the first profession of faith in Jesus as Messiah from the mouth of a woman (*evangeliste*).

3. *The Christian Messiah*

There remain some texts that speak of Jesus as Messiah from a Christian viewpoint. In the first chapter, we can recognise a journey of faith in Jesus the Messiah. At the prompting of John the Baptist, two disciples (Andrew and another who is not named but who, for many, is John) approach Jesus and spend a whole evening with him. Thereupon, Andrew finds his brother Simon and says to him: 'We have found the Messiah (which means "Christ"' (Jn 1:41). After this, Jesus finds Philip and calls him to follow him. In his turn, Philip then finds Nathaniel and says to him: 'We have found him of whom Moses in the law and also the prophets wrote' (1:45). Nathaniel – to whom Jesus reveals his most personal experiences – confesses: 'Rabbi, you are the Son of God; you are the King of Israel' (1:49). The chapter closes with a revelation of Jesus as the Son of Man (1:51). For the theme of Jesus as Messiah, it is important to see the progression from the confession of Andrew (Jesus is the Messiah) to that of Nathaniel which links the profession of Jesus as 'King of Israel' (Messiah) with that of Jesus as 'Son of God'. This connection will reappear in the course of the Fourth Gospel.

Before presenting the succeeding texts, it is a good idea to reflect briefly on the significance of the Christological title 'Son of God'. Today a twofold linguistic origin for such a title is recognised. On the one hand, the title has its antecedents in the Biblical tradition. Scholars refer to Ps 2:7 where God says to the king (his 'anointed'); 'You are my son, today I have begotten you'. Probably we are faced here with an adoption formula like those found in some texts from the kingdoms bordering on Israel. It is evident that there is no question here of a physical descent of the king from God. In Hos 11:1, it is the whole people of Israel that is called 'son' of God: 'When Israel was a child, I loved him; and out of Egypt I called my son'. Also in this case, the sonship is not physical or metaphysical but spiritual. The other line from which one can trace to a certain extent the divine sonship of Jesus is the Hellenistic world. The ancient mythology knows various types of descent of human beings from the gods. The heroes are born in this way. John, who, with the early Church, shares the conviction of faith in the divine Sonship of Jesus, has undergone the influence of this double cultural world but has not arrived at faith in Jesus the messiah and Son of God by means of this double tradition. Faith comes from the encounter with Jesus and from hearing: for John, from the beholding the signs of Jesus (cf Jn 2:11) and from the hearing of his words.

After this clarification, we can return to the passages in the Fourth Gospel that speak of Jesus as Messiah and 'Son of God' in a Christian sense. After the profession of faith by the Samaritan Woman, we find another example in the mouth of a woman in Jn 11:27. Martha had gone to meet Jesus after the death of her brother to get him to join in her mourning and sadness. Step by step, Jesus leads her to the confession of her faith in the resurrection of the dead and to the recognition that he himself is 'the resurrection and the life' (11:25). Questioned about her faith, Martha replies: 'Yes, Lord; I believe that you are the Christ, the Son of God, he who is coming into the world' (11:27).

Scholars have noted that Martha's profession of faith corresponds verbally to that which appears as the aim of the whole of the Fourth Gospel at its first conclusion in Jn 20:30f: 'Now Jesus did many other signs in the presence of the disciples, which are not written in this book; but these are written that you may believe that Jesus is the Christ, the Son of God, and that believing you may have life in his name'. Rensberger, in his article, highlights the importance of three elements which go to make up Martha's faith: Jesus the Messiah – Son of God – the one who is to come into the world. The final element refers to the sending of Jesus by the Father.

It is precisely because of this special sending by the Father that Jesus distinguishes himself from other kings and from the messianic expectations of Israel. The people hail him as 'he who comes in the name of the Lord, the king of Israel' (12:13), but they stay within the traditional perspective. Jesus enters into his own city fulfilling the prophecy of Zechariah: 'Fear not, daughter of Zion! Behold, your king is coming, sitting upon an ass's colt' (12:15). It is possible to make out a truly messianic dimension in this scene, but it lacks that typically Johannine element.

Also during the trial of Jesus, he remains for the Jews a pretender, like others, to the throne and thus a source of competition to the Emperor. It is exactly for this reason that Pilate is induced to condemn him to death on the cross (Jn 19:12-15). The legend over his cross indicates the cause of his execution: 'Jesus of Nazareth, the King of the

Jews' (Jn 19:19). This evokes the protest of the chief priests, but the text remains as it stands. Here we have a final example of 'Johannine irony': for the passers-by, Jesus is thought to be only the King of the Jews; for believers, however, Jesus is their king and the Saviour of the world (cf Jn 4:42).

The Johannine viewpoint appears clearly in the central scene of the trial of Jesus before the Romans. To the question whether he is 'the King of the Jews' (Jn 18:33), Jesus responds affirmatively, but adds that his kingdom is not of this world and that he has come into the world to bear witness to the truth (18:37). Jesus is king as revealer of the Father. It is for this that he has come into the world. Whoever is of the truth, listens to his voice.

In two passages, the Johannine vision summarises, and at the same time is enclosed in professions of faith of the early Christian communities. In a certain sense, these two passages form a frame around the public life of Jesus before his Passion. At the end of the Prologue, we read: 'For the law was given through Moses; grace and truth came through Jesus Christ' (1:17) and, in the final prayer of Jesus: 'This is eternal life: that they know you, the only true God and Jesus Christ whom you have sent' (17:3).

Lecture XVI

The Son of Man

Bibliography:

C. H. DODD, *The Interpretation of the Fourth Gospel*, Cambridge: University Press 1953; F. J. MOLONEY, *The Johannine Son of Man*, Rome: LAS 1976; C. K. BARRETT, *The Gospel according to St John*, London: SPCK ²1978; W. THÜSING, *Die Erhöhung und Verherrlichung Jesu im Johannesevangelium* (NTA 21,1-2), Münster: Aschendorff ³1979; J. BLANK, *Das Evangelium nach Johannes I* (GSL.NT 4.1a), Düsseldorf: Patmos 1981; F. HAHN, 'υἱός', *EDNT* III (1993) 381-392: 387-391; X. LÉON-DUFOUR, *Lecture de l'évangile selon Jean I* (Parole de Dieu), Paris: du Seuil 1987; R. FABRIS, *Giovanni* (Commenti biblici), Rome: Borla 1992; Y. SIMOENS, *Selon Jean*, Bruxelles: IET 1997; G. R. BEASLEY-MURRAY, *John* (WBC 36), Dallas, Texas: Word Books Publisher 1998.

1. *A controversial topic*

Throughout the twentieth century, the theme of the Johannine Son of Man was treated according to various perspectives in accordance with the different approaches of those researching the question. For a long time, particularly within liberal Protestant research in Germany, the hypothesis of a gnostic myth of the Primordial Man dominated the scene. R. Bultmann had encountered this myth in the Gnostic texts of the Mandaeans and had sought to utilise it for the interpretation of the Johannine Son of Man. According to this myth, the fall of humanity had led also to its dispersal. A Primordial Man who had descended among men would then have led them back again to unity and to the higher world by means of his esoteric revelation. The existence of this myth has been put in question subsequently by other scholars, among them by C. Colpe in his book *Die religionsgeschichtliche Schule*,[39] and in his article on the Son of Man in the *TDNT* (Vol 8, pp 400-477). The

---

[39] FRLANT 78, Göttingen, Vandenhoeck & Ruprecht 1961.

texts adduced by Bultmann were too late, and the elements of the so-called Myth of the Primordial Man (*Urmensch*) had to be sought in various documents of different, and not infrequently distant, provenance. In his commentary (Vol I, English edition pp 538-542), R. Schnackenburg took up again the theme of the Johannine Son of Man. He revealed himself to be still under the influence of Bultmann but was seeking to open new horizons for the theme, above all Biblical and apocalyptic ones. The majority of authors of recent years have followed along these lines (cf, *supra*, bibliography).

2. *The Son of Man in John*

R. Schnackenburg[40] summarises in various groups the thirteen Johannine passages which speak of the Son of Man. The first three groups can be defined thus:

– the Son of Man descended from heaven who ascends there again (3:13;6:62)

– the 'exaltation' of the Son of Man (3:14; 8:28; 12:34c)

– the 'glorification' of the Son of Man (11:4; 12:23; 13:31f).

The author sees a closeness between the themes of the exaltation and the glorification of the Son of Man. We shall return to this point.

A further group of texts is found in the Bread of Life Discourse in Jn 6. In these, Jesus speaks of the bread that has come from heaven which the Son of Man will give to his own to eat (6:27) and which is He himself according to the 'Eucharistic' section of this discourse (6:53): it is necessary to eat the flesh of the Son of Man and to drink his blood to have life in oneself. These passages are close to the others which we met with above (cf the echo of 3:13 and 6:62) regarding the Son of Man who descends from heaven and returns there.

In a further two passages, the expression 'Son of Man' is used almost as if it were a title. In 9:35-6 and 12:34, the crowd, or someone from the crowd, asks who is that 'Son of Man'. The question is one

---

[40] *The Gospel according to St John,* I, New York: Crossroad 1982, 530.

about the messiah (cf 12:34c) who is, according to the evangelist, the Son of Man.[41]

Jn 1:51, where the Son of Man on earth is seen in constant union with God, remains an exception. In its context, this passage is to be set within the group of passages about the descending and ascending Son of Man.[42] The 'ladder' on which the angels ascend and descend upon him is the symbol of this divine origin and status.

Jn 5:27 lies outside this perspective. The text speaks of 'a Son of Man' as of someone who will execute a judgement. As will be seen, this text is closer to the Synoptic and apocalyptic tradition. In John, however, this judgement is integrated into the eschatological future and, at the same time, already 'realised': thus the Son of Man has also a role that is not only future.

3. The traditional background of the Johannine Son of Man

The title 'Son of Man' in John has its roots in the early Christian tradition, prescinding from the fact that the evangelist may have known the Synoptic Gospels directly or by means of oral traditions. In the Synoptic Gospels, scholars distinguish three contexts in which Son of Man sayings are found (always on the mouth of Jesus):[43]

– sayings about the Son of man present on earth
– sayings about the Son of Man who has to suffer, die and rise from the dead
– sayings about the Son of Man who will be exalted and will come again in judgement.

The closest contacts are those between the Johannine Son of Man and the Synoptic tradition concerning the Son of man who must suffer, die and rise again. In the Synoptic Gospels, these sayings of Jesus are found above all in the section Mk 8:27-10:52 which begins with Peter's Confession and the first prediction of the future Passion, Death and Resurrection of Jesus (Mk 8:31 parr). From this moment, the

---

[41] SCHNACKENBURG, 531
[42] Ibid.
[43] Cf. F. HAHN, loc. cit., 388.

confession of Jesus the Messiah, is transformed into faith in Jesus the Son of Man, suffering but victorious in the cross and resurrection.

John has taken this central thought but has transformed it with his perspective of the Son of Man 'lifted up' and 'glorified', as we shall see in section (D). It can be said that he has combined the two last aspects listed above making the glory of the Risen One to shine in the Exaltation on the cross.

B) The apocalyptic tradition

The early Christian tradition about the Son of Man finds its roots in the apocalyptic tradition. The specialists in this field are agreed on the fact that the address 'Son of man', which is employed repeatedly in the Book of Ezekiel (2:1; 3:1 etc) did not have any influence on the Johannine (or indeed New Testament) Son of Man. In John, 'Son of Man' is not used as a form of address, but always in the third person. Besides, in Ezekiel, this expression does not mean anything other than a human being and does not have any of the characteristics belonging to titles of excellence.

Another attempt which can be made to explain the Johannine and, again, the other NT uses Son of Man has recourse to Semitic linguistics and seeks to see in this expression a way of speaking which a person may use to indicate himself (*bar nasha* = *hahu' gabra*). This proposal also is of little use in explaining the Johannine Son of Man because in the majority of cases Jesus speaks of the Son of Man with reference to his destiny and to his mission.

The root of the Son of Man of the gospels seems to be located in the Book of Daniel 7:13f. The prophet describes a vision in which various 'animal' empires succeed one another until the coming of 'one like a son of man'. The successor to the pagan, sub-human empires is an empire instituted by God that has a truly human face. The promised figure has traits that are simultaneously collective and individual. To the Son of Man thus promised, who comes on the clouds of heaven, justice is entrusted.

As time goes on, this figure of the apocalyptic Son of Man has an influence on Jewish and early Christian literature. In the *Fourth Book of Ezra* (13:3, 5, 12), a 'Man' is named who first comes up out of the sea and then comes down from a mountain in order to judge the people.

The same kind of figure reappears in the *First Book of Enoch*, in Chapters 37-71, the 'Similitudes of Enoch'. This part of the Enochian collection seems to be the most recent because no trace of it has been found at Qumran. Thus it should be dated in the second half of the first century AD. In this document, the 'Son of Man' has an important and dominant role. Enoch sees the future judgement of the wicked and the rebellious nations. This judgement is entrusted to the Son of Man; he receives a new name, and the just will live with him in the world to come, a world of peace (cf *1 En* 46:3; 62:14; 63:11; 69:27, 29; 70:1; 71:17).

The 'Son of Man' is also called 'the Chosen One' of God (48:6; 49:2, 4; 51:3, 5; 52:6, 9; 53:6; 55:4; 61:5, 8) and, once, 'the Messiah' (52:4). The title of Chosen One makes one think of the Isaianic figure of the Servant of God (42:1). This impression is strengthened by the fact that it is said of the Son of Man that he will be a 'light of the Gentiles' (48:4) – an expression taken from the First Servant Song (Is 42:6). These observations are of considerable importance for the closeness of the title of 'Son of Man' and 'Servant of God' in John (see below, section (D).

In the Fourth Gospel, the idea of the Son of Man who executes judgement is taken up in 5:7. Precisely because the evangelist speaks here of '*a* Son of man' (without the definite article), it is considered by exegetes as proof of the direct literary dependence of John on Daniel.

C) The Wisdom tradition

In no part of Scripture does divine Wisdom have a direct connection with the 'Son of Man'. Scholars refer to Wisdom only for the structural resemblance between the destiny of Wisdom and that of the Johannine Son of Man.

For the 'myth' of the divine Wisdom which (pre-existent or not) descends from God and seeks its dwelling among men, as background to the Johannine theme of the coming of the divine Logos, cf above, Lecture VII. The same idea of the coming of Wisdom seems to have also exercised an influence on the Johannine theology of the coming of the Son of Man. Cf the texts above, section 2 cited in support of this idea (Jn 3:13; 6:62) and Schnackenburg. To the texts taken from the canonical Wisdom literature, we could add further *1 En* 42.

In a certain sense, this idea of the descent and return of the Divine Logos appears even central for the Fourth Gospel, and Schnackenburg takes it as his framework of discussion for the study of the Johannine texts about the Son of Man.

D) The tradition of the Servant of God

Scholars have hesitated a great deal before accepting a direct influence of the Servant Songs of Is 42-53 on the Johannine texts that speak of the Son of Man. On the one hand, the title of 'Servant of God' is absent from the Fourth Gospel; on the other hand, above all for the school of Bultmann, the alternative of the Gnostic myth of the Primordial Man presents itself. As has been seen (*supra*, section 1), this hypothesis appears to have been abandoned today and the importance of the Isaianic Servant of God for the Johannine concept of the Son of Man has been discovered, al least in the Anglican and catholic exegetical literature of recent years.

Generally speaking, scholars treat the question of the link between the Son of Man and the Servant in connection with the exegesis of Jn 3:13f. Here, for the first time, the 'Son of Man' who will be lifted up is spoken of (3:14). The expression "ὑψωθήσεται" evokes Is 52:13 LXX, where it is said of the Servant: "ὑψωθήσεται καὶ δοξασθήσεται σφόδρα". We have dealt with this connection in our eleventh lecture with a reference to my article: 'Greeks come to see Jesus (Jn 12:20f)' in *Bibl* 71 (1990) 334-347 and the German version of this article. In fact, Is 52:13 LXX is the only verse in the LXX in which the two verbs are found together with the exception of Ps 36:20 where it is said of the enemies of God that they will be raised up and glorified before their fall!

The interpreters of Jn 3 often notice only the linguistic affinity of Jn 3:14 with Is 52:13 LXX; some reckon only with the possibility of the influence of the verse from Isaiah on that from John.[44]

One reason why the importance of the verse from Isaiah for the Johannine theology of the Servant/Son of Man has not been noticed is because W. Thüsing, in his detailed monograph. had separated the predicates of being 'lifted up' and 'glorified'. Thüsing saw the 'lifting up' of Jesus as something that happened on the cross, and his 'glorification' in the resurrection and return to the Father.

This stance has, however, been rejected subsequently, and contemporary writers – from Schnackenburg on – see a unity between the 'lifting up' and the 'glorification' of Jesus. In fact, Jesus is at one and the same time both lifted up on the cross and raised up to the Father. This is an example of Johannine 'irony' in which a reality of this world serves as a mirror for another reality, not of this world, which can be very different, even opposed to, the appearance.

It is fitting to read the Johannine texts on the 'lifting up' and on the 'glorification' of the Son of Man as a series, from 3:14, passing through 8:28, up to Chapter 12 where the theology of the lifted up and glorified Son of Man finds its culmination. Above all, in this chapter, the thematic unity of the Son of Man and the Servant in John is revealed. From this unity there also results the soteriological importance of the figure of the Son of Man in the Fourth Gospel.

---

[44] Thus F. J. MOLONEY, *Son of Man*, 63; R. FABRIS, *Giovanni*, 253.

Lecture XVII

The Hour

Bibliography:

G. FERRARO, L'"Ora" di Cristo nel Quarto Vangelo (Aloisiana, 10), Rome: Herder 1974; G. DELLING, 'ὥρα', *TDNT* IX (1974) 675-681; H. GIESEN, 'ὥρα', *EDNT* III (1993) 506-508; J. BEUTLER, 'Die Stunde Jesu im Johannesevangelium', *BiKi* 52 (1997) 25-27 = ID., *Studien zu den johanneischen Schriften* (SBAB 25), Stuttgart: Katholisches Bibelwerk 1998, 317-322; J. FREY, *Die johanneische Eschatologie* III (WUNT 117), Tübingen: Mohr – Siebeck 2000.

1. The Eschatological Hour in the literary environment of John's Gospel

A) Old Testament

The fact that the majority of texts of the Old Testament were written in Hebrew or Aramaic makes it difficult to trace a direct line between these texts and those of the New Testament. The Hebrew word that matches the Greek word 'ὥρα' is עֵת. The two words share the fact that they both mean 'fixed time' rather than 'hour' (Delling). In this sense, the concept recurs repeatedly in the Old Testament.

An eschatological-apocalyptic usage occurs for the first time in the Book of Daniel.[45] In Dan 7:13, the 'Son of Man' to whom the judgement has been entrusted was introduced (cf *supra*, Lecture XVI). In Chapters 11 and 12 the judgement which the Son of Man will execute is announced. In this connection, the concept 'hour' also occurs (Dan 11:35, 40, 45; 12:1). Subsequently it is replaced by that of 'the day' (12:1). Both concepts stand for the Hebrew עֵת[46]. The expression serves, first of all, to designate the final period before the arrival of the judge and, afterwards to introduce his time itself.

---

[45] Cf. G. FERRARO, chap. 4.
[46] Ferraro, 77.

B) Apocalyptic Literature outside the Old Testament

Once again we are faced with the linguistic problem. The sequence
of ages established by God in the course of the history of salvation is
fundamental for apocalyptic literature. By contrast, those texts which
speak of the 'hour' are rare. The concept of the 'day' seems to have
been more accepted, something which seems to have been equivalent to
the 'hour' already in Daniel. Thus, the *Fourth Book of Ezra* speaks
repeatedly of the future 'days' when history shall be fulfilled (6:17;
10:6; 13:29; 16:17, 32, 75) and of the 'day' of judgement (7:43; 12:34).

In the Qumran documents we find equivalent formulas (cf Delling,
679): הקץ האחרון in 1QpHab 7:7, 12; cf. 1QS 4:16f for 'the last
days'.

C) The New Testament outside John

The New Testament knows of 'the hour' of the divine eschatological intervention, whether in the negative sense of the testing by the
devil and his power, or with the positive slant of time of divine grace.
The word is found in this latter sense in the Letter to the Romans
(13:11): 'Besides this you know what hour it is (καιρός), how it is full
time (ὥρα) now for you to wake from sleep. For salvation is nearer to
us now than when we first believed'.

The 'hour' of the eschatological conflict appears in the scene of the
prayer of Jesus in the Garden of Gethsemane according to Mk 14:32-42
par. In this scene, Jesus prays to the Father that 'the hour' may pass
(Mk 14:35). Peter is rebuked for not having been able to watch with the
Lord for even one hour (14:38). In the end, Jesus gets up from the
ground and says to the disciples: 'The hour is come; the Son of Man is
betrayed into the hands of sinners' (14:41).

In his Eschatological Discourse, Jesus prepares the disciples for the
future trials in the final conflict with the forces of evil. The disciples
will be brought before tribunals. 'When they bring you to trial and
deliver you up, do not be anxious beforehand what you are to say; but
say whatever is given you in that hour, for it is not you who speak, but

the Holy Spirit' (Mk 13:11). At the end of the discourse, Jesus replies to the question (albeit tacit) concerning the identification of that final age of history with the words: 'But of that day or that hour no one knows, not even the angels in heaven, nor the Son, but only the Father' (Mk 13:32).

In a formula, which is certainly traditional, the First Letter of John says twice: 'It is the last hour' (1 Jn 2:18). The concept of the eschatological hour also pervades the Apocalypse of John (3:3, 10; 9:15; 11:13; 14:7, 15; the judgement on Babylon is to be 'in an hour' 17:10; 18:10, 17, 19).

It seems legitimate, therefore, to see the eschatological 'hour' in John's Gospel as the expression of a vocabulary and concept that was traditional.

2. *The Hour in John's Gospel*

A) Hours of the day

In some parts of the Fourth Gospel, 'the hour' simply signifies a time of the day. However, this time has always a meaning for faith. The first example of the use of the word is found in Jn 1:39. The first two disciples have met with Jesus for the first time. According to the text, after many years, they still remember: 'It was about the eleventh hour'. In Jn 4:6 mention is made of Jesus sitting at Jacob's Well. The evangelist comments: 'It was about the sixth hour', about midday, therefore, the hour of the greatest heat and the fiercest thirst – something important for the sequel. In the account of the healing of the centurion's son, the hour of Jesus' words which announce the healing coincides with that of the healing itself (Jn 4:52f). During the dialogue between Jesus and his disciples before his final ascent to Jerusalem, he remarks that his hours are numbered: he can neither lengthen nor shorten the period of life allotted to him by the Father: 'Are there not twelve hours in the day?' (Jn 11:9). In the Passion Narrative, the day and the hour in which Pilate takes the decision to put Jesus to death are recorded: 'It was the Day of Preparation of the Passover; it was about the sixth hour' (Jn 19:14). Exegetes see in this chronological note a possible reference to the hour of the slaughter of the Paschal lambs according to Jewish tradition. The final occurrence of this concept of the 'hour' as a time of day comes in Jn 19:27. Here too, the chronological indication has a deeper sense: from the 'hour' in which Jesus confided his mother to the Beloved Disciple and the Beloved Disciple to his mother, that disciple took her into his own home. A new relationship is created, and one open to a symbolical interpretation.

B) The hour of eschatological worship

During his conversation with the Samaritan Woman, Jesus announces a future time, a time that has already begun, when there will be a new kind of worship of God which will be on neither this mountain nor that (Gerizim or Zion): 'Woman, believe me, the hour is coming when neither on this mountain nor in Jerusalem will you worship the Father' (Jn 4:21). This declaration is clarified in the following: 'The hour is coming, and now is, when the true worshipers will worship the Father in spirit and truth' (4:23). While Jesus' first announcement still refers to a future hour, the second sees 'the hour' as having already arrived and begun. The commentators see in this formula a characteristic expression of Johannine eschatology. In Jesus, the eschatological fulfillment of the history of salvation has already arrived or at least begun. There remains a tension between the 'already' and the 'not yet'. The connection between the announcement of the future cult and the concept of the 'hour' is Johannine and does not seem to depend on the Old Testament tradition. For a future cult which is not necessarily on Mount Zion, scholars make reference to Is 66:1 and Mal 1:11[47]

C) The hour of the resurrection of the dead and of the judgment

The closest connection with the Biblical and Jewish tradition in the use of the concept of 'hour' is found in Jn 5:25-29. It is the hour of judgment. Jesus is replying to the accusation of the Jews that he has violated the Sabbath by curing a paralytic on this day, and he does this with a reference to his activity which is in close union with that of the Father (Jn 5:19-30). Just as the Father gives life and judges every day,

---

[47] Cf the margin of Nestle-Aland.

even on the Sabbath, the Son does likewise. Scholars observe the parallelism between verses 25 and 28f:

Jn 5:25	Jn 5:28f
ἔρχεται ὥρα	ἔρχεται ὥρα
καὶ νῦν ἐστιν	--
ὅτε οἱ νεκροὶ	ἐν ᾗ πάντες οἱ ἐν τοῖς μνημείοις
ἀκούσουσιν τῆς φωνῆς	ἀκούσουσιν τῆς φωνῆς
τοῦ υἱοῦ τοῦ θεοῦ	αὐτοῦ
καὶ οἱ ἀκούσαντες ζήσουσιν	καὶ ἐκπορεύσονται οἱ τὰ ἀγαθὰ ποιήσαντες εἰς ἀνάστασιν ζωῆς, οἱ δὲ τὰ φαῦλα πράξαντες εἰς ἀνάστασιν κρίσεως

On the one hand, the two texts are like each other; on the other, there is also a notable difference between them. In the first instance, Jesus announces the arrival of the hour of the resurrection as here and now; in the second, the resurrection will take place only in the future. There are also other differences: in the first case, the resurrection is granted to those who hear the voice of the Son of God; in the second, there is a future resurrection – to life, for those who have done good works, or to judgement for those whose works are evil.

Scholars frequently try to find a diachronic solution for this difference of viewpoint. One possibility consists in the attribution of the more 'primitive' model of vv 28f to a first redaction of John's Gospel and of the more 'advanced' model of v 25 to a second hand. [48] The opposite proposal is that of R. Bultmann in his commentary. According to him, Jn 5:25 is the work of the evangelist. Verses 28f were added by the 'ecclesiastical redactor' who wanted to adapt the bold positions of the evangelist to the faith of the community at the end of the first century AD with a new emphasis on future eschatology and on judgement according to works. This proposal has been followed subsequently by various authors, catholic as well as protestant. [49]

---

[48] This is, for example, the proposal of M.-É. BOISMARD in *RB* 68 (1961) 507-524.

[49] The school of G. Richter and J. Hainz.

Recently the problem has been treated again thoroughly (and, as it seems, successfully) by J. Frey in his work which we have cited – the third volume of a monumental study which was published in the brief period of three years between 1997 and 2000. The author is a former pupil of Martin Hengel and comes from Tübingen where the exegesis of Bultmann's Marburg school has always been followed with a critical eye. According to Frey, the two texts listed above (in the table) represent two Johannine traditions inserted and reworked by the evangelist. The origin of the first passage in the tradition is observed because of the formula of introduction 'Truly, truly, I say to you', and from the grammatical change from the third to the first person. Also the title of 'Son of God' seems to be traditional; it is not attested in the context. The evangelist would have taken the verse from the homiletic tradition of his community and added the aspect typical of his own theology 'καὶ νῦν ἐστιν' (in this Frey is coming close to the position of Bultmann). Behind these words can be found Dan 7:13f and 12:1-3 in a much elaborated form. It is not good works or bad that are decisive in the resurrection; what is decisive is the hearing of the voice of the Son of God (in faith). The 'dead' are not those who are physically dead but those who have need of the divine life that is granted by Jesus who reveals the Father. This courageous reinterpretation of Jewish belief in the final resurrection could have given rise to doubts even among the believers of the Johannine community. For this reason, the evangelist adds another version of the proclamation of the future life, one that is nearer to the traditional faith. Jesus is presented as the giver of life and the judge by recourse to the tradition of Daniel (vv 26f), and, as a result, the announcement of the future life is reformulated. The introduction 'Do not marvel at this' has the significance of leading the readers to find a reason for faith in Jesus who is the one to cause the dead to rise and to give life. This reason is found in the divine announcement of a future resurrection of the dead and of a future judgement. Except that John also changes this traditional faith: it is not 'the dead' (already defined in another way in v 25) who rise, but 'those who are in the tombs', the physically dead. The wording is taken from Is 26:19 LXX. By contrast with the Book of Daniel, all rise, not just many, and only the wicked will have to undergo the judgement. So there is not a universal judgement in the end. With these modifications, the evangelist simultaneously safeguards the tradition and the faith conviction of his community.

D) The hour of Jesus

The most characteristic use of the concept of 'hour' in the Fourth Gospel is that which speaks of the hour of Jesus. The expression occurs for the first time in Jn 2:4. Here, the manifestation of the glory of Jesus (cf 2:11) is connected with his 'hour'. During the controversies of Chapters 5-10, twice it is made known that Jesus could not yet be arrested or executed because his hour had not yet come (7:30; 8:20). After the arrival of the Greeks, this hour has thenceforth arrived (12:23, 27; 13:1; 17:1. This hour is the glorification of Jesus as Son of Man and Servant of God (12:23, 27f; 17:1, cf, *supra* Lectures XI and XVI).

E) The hour of the Church

The hour of Jesus is prolonged in the hour of the disciples. The first Farewell Discourse of Jesus on Jn 14 has a Christological character: Jesus is leaving his own, but he is not abandoning and he will return among them. In the second and third Farewell Discourse (Jn 15:1-16:4a and 16:4b-33), the disciples are more at the centre of Jesus' teaching. According to Jn 16:2, 4, the hour of future persecution, even persecution in the name of God, will come. Later, the concept of the hour is taken up again and developed with the image of the woman in travail (16:21). The woman is distressed during the actual childbearing but soon full of joy once her hour has come. With Jesus' departure, a new period of his revelation of the Father is beginning, an 'hour' in which he will not speak any longer in parables, but openly (16:25). First, however, the hour of the scattering of the disciples has to come (16:32), an hour announced by the prophet Zechariah (13:7). Again, then, we have in John a 'variations on a theme'. The eschatological hour of judgement and resurrection, taken from Daniel, is taken up under various aspects: liturgical, Christological and ecclesial.

Lecture XVIII

Testimony

Bibliography:

J. BEUTLER, *Martyria. Traditionsgeschichtliche Untersuchungen zum Zeugnisthema bei Johannes* (FTS 10), Frankfurt a. M.: Knecht 1972; ID., 'μαρτυρέω - μαρτυρία - μάρτυς', *EDNT* II (1991) 389-395; ID., 'Zeuge, Zeugnis, Zeugenschaft I. Biblisch', *LThK³* 10 (2001) 1440-1442.

The idea of 'testimony' belongs with the central ideas of the Fourth Gospel. We can distinguish three uses of this idea.

1. *The testimony in favour of Jesus*

In a first group of texts, various 'witnesses' or rather 'testimonies' for Jesus are found in the Fourth Gospel. The characteristic construction is 'μαρτυρέω περί τινος' with genitive of the person. Named as 'witnesses' for Jesus are:
- John the Baptist (Jn 1:7f, 15, 19, 32, 34; cf 3:26; 5:33)
- the Scriptures (Jn 5:39)
- the Father (Jn 5:32, 37; 8:18)
- the works of Jesus which the Father has granted him to accomplish (Jn 5:36; 10:25)
- Jesus himself (8:14, 18)
- The Spirit-Paraclete (15:26)
- The disciples (15:27)

In the Prologue, John the Baptist is introduced as one who bears witness to the light without being the light (Jn 1:7f, cf 1:15). Later, his testimony can be called testimony on behalf of the truth (5:33). Christ is always the one about whom John bears witness. During the time of the public life of Jesus, John remains the most important human witness on his behalf. Naming him for the last time in 10:40-42, the evangelist is at the same time providing a frame for the public life. In the period which begins with the death and resurrection of Jesus, the Spirit and the disciples will take his place (cf 15:26f).

The theme of the testimony in favour of Jesus is treated at more length in the Fourth Gospel in the sections 5:31-40 and 8:12-20. In the first section, Jesus accepts the position of his enemies concerning the lack of validity in his witness in favour of himself. For this reason, he refers to other witnesses such as John the Baptist, the Father, the works granted to him by the Father and the Scriptures. In the second section, Jn 8:12-20, Jesus contradicts the position of his enemies and recognises the validity of his testimony about himself: since the Law (Num 35:30; Deut 17:6; 19:15) recognises the validity of two witnesses, his own testimony together with that of the Father provides sufficient basis for faith in him.

From the beginning of the last century, scholars and exegetes have drawn attention to the forensic language of the Fourth Gospel. Beside 'testimony', one finds also the concepts of 'judgement', 'Paraclete' (Advocate) and 'convicting' (ἐλέγχειν). Cf the commentary on John of W. Heitmüller (1918[3]) and the little work of W. Wrede, *Charakter und Tendenz des Johannesevangeliums*[50] It is possible to recognise in the Fourth Gospel a 'great trial' of Jesus and his claim to be the One sent from God. In his favour, Jesus refers to the witnesses listed above. In the end it will not be him who is judged but the world which accuses him.

For this trial, some authors[51] have made reference to the legal process between God and the pagan divinities in some passages of the Old Testament (cf Is 43:9f, 12; 44:8) where Israel appears as witness. However, this tradition is rather distant from the logic of the Fourth Gospel. Nearer to the Johannine lawsuit are the texts of the Hellenistic Judaism of the time of the Fourth Evangelist. Philo of Alexandria is aware of a theological use of the concept of divine 'testimony'. In one text (*Leg All* II 55), he refers to the Greek expression 'σκηνὴ τοῦ μαρτυρίου' in Ex 33:7 which, in Greek, means 'tent of the testimony' (the original Hebrew means rather 'tent of meeting'). Philo sees in this Greek expression a reference to a divine witness for the exit of the soul that loves God from the body to live a life full of virtue. The text of the

---

[50] Tübingen-Leipzig 1903.
[51] Such as, for example, H. Stratmann in *TDNT*.

Bible does not say who had called this tent ' tent of the testimony' ἵνα
συγκινηθεῖσα ἡ ψυχὴ σκέψηται, τίς ὁ μαρτυρῶν ταῖς φιλαρέτοις
διανοίαις ἐστί.[52] Thus the souls that love virtue receive a divine
testimony.

In another text, Philo speaks of the divine testimony in the context
of the Exodus and of the signs which accompany Israel's leaving
Egypt. This text is an apology for Judaism in the form of a biography of
Moses (*De Vita Moysis*). In the Second Book, Philo speaks of the
miracle of the manna, and of the fact that that every Friday, a double
quantity was given to the Israelites so that they would not need to
collect anything on the Sabbath.[53] 2.263 ὅπερ ἀδηλούμενον ἐπιθειάσας
ἀνέφηνε 2.264 λογίῳ μαρτυρηθέντι διὰ σημείου τινὸς ἐναργοῦς. τὸ δὲ
σημεῖον τοιοῦτον ἦν· ἐλάττων μὲν ἀπ' ἀέρος ἐγίνετο ἡ φορὰ ταῖς
προτέραις ἡμέραις τῆς τροφῆς, τότε δ' αὖ διπλασίων· καὶ ταῖς μὲν
προτέραις εἴ τι κατελείφθη, λειβόμενον ἐτήκετο μέχρι τοῦ παντελῶς
εἰς νοτίδα μεταβαλὸν ἀναλωθῆναι, τότε δ'οὐδεμίαν ἐνδεχόμενον τροφὴν
ἐν ὁμοίῳ διέμενεν· εφ' οἷς ἀγγελλομένοις ἅμα καὶ ὁρωμένοις
καταπλαγεὶς Μωυσῆς οὐκ 2.265 ἐστοχάσατο μᾶλλον ἢ θεοφορηθεὶς
ἐθέσπισε τὴν ἐβδόμην.

The English translation is as follows: 'This hidden truth Moses,
under inspiration, revealed in an announcement to which a manifest
sign gave testimony. This sign was as follows: the shower of food from
the air was less on the first days, but on later day was doubled; and on
those first days anything left melted and was dissolved till, after turning
completely into moisture, it disappeared; but on that later day it
admitted no change and remained just as it had been'.[54]

The miracle of which the text speaks at the beginning is more
precisely a 'sign' (σνμεῖον). This 'sign' bears witness to the institution
of the Sabbath during the Exodus and confirms the mission of Moses

---

[52] Cf Philo vol I in LCL ed F. H. Colson and G. H. Whittaker, Cambridge MA: HUP,
1929, pp 258-259. The translation runs: 'in order that the soul may be stirred up to
consider who it is that bears witness to virtue-loving minds'.
[53] The quotation is drawn from the *Thesaurus Linguae graecae*
[54] Cf Philo Vol 6 with an English translation by F. H. Colson (LCL), Cambridge MA:
HUP, 1935, pp 580-583.

indirectly. With these ideas, we find ourselves close to the vocabulary and thought of John. A difference will be noticed in the fact that John speaks of the testimony of the works (ἔργα) performed by Jesus and granted to him by the Father for that purpose (cf Jn 5:36; 10:25). The language of Philo is attested in Heb 2:4 and Acts 14:3. John comes close to this language in Jn 2:11 – the disciples see Jesus' 'signs' and believe on him.

In another, similar text (*De Vita Moysis* II), Philo cites Moses who addresses the Israelites after the revolt of Korah (Num 16). The death of the rebels will show whether Moses was in the right or not: Mos 2.281.3 ἐπικριθήσεται δὲ τοῦτο τῇ τοῦ βίου τελευτῇ· εἰ μὲν γὰρ θάνατον ἐνδέξονται τὸν κατὰ φύσιν, πέπλασμαι τὰ λόγια, εἰ δὲ καινόν τινα καὶ παρηλλαγμένον, τὸ φιλάληθές μοι μαρτυρηθήσεται. 'This matter will be judged by the manner of their latter end. If the death they meet is in the ordinary course of nature, my oracles are a false invention; but, if it be of a new and different kind, my truthfulness will be attested.'[55]

The other author who comes from the Jewish-Hellenistic environment of the period is Josephus. Like Philo, this author speaks of the divine 'testimony' in an apologetic writing (*Against Apion* II 53).[56] The High Priest Onias defends Cleopatra from a usurper. The usurper then makes some elephants drunk so that they will attack and kill the Jews. But these animals do not touch the Jews. Rather, they attack the latter's enemies. The author sees in this a divine testimony: 'Testis autem Deus iustititiae eius manifestus est.'

2. *The testimony of Jesus*

In some texts of the Fourth Gospel, Jesus himself appears as the one who gives the testimony. The construction is μαρτυρέω τι. In the dialogue with Nicodemus, Jesus says: 'We speak of what we know, and bear witness to what we have seen; but you do not receive our testimony' (Jn 3:11). The same formula recurs in Jn 3:31f: 'He who

---

[55] Philo Vol 6 as in previous note, pp 590-591.
[56] Cf JOSEPHUS, *Life. Against Apion*, ed. H. St. J. Thackeray, Cambridge, Massachusetts: HUP, 1926, p 314.

comes from above is above all... He bears witness to what he has seen and heard, yet no one receives his testimony'.

With this idea we find ourselves once more in the apocalyptic environment. The Apocalypse of John has similar texts. The seer testifies to 'what he saw: the testimony of God and the word of Jesus' (1:2). The content of the book is to be 'testified to' by the angel to the community (22:16) just as it has been 'testified to' by Jesus himself (22:20).

Similar expressions and ideas are found in Jewish apocalyptic. The *Second Book of Enoch* begins thus:[57] 'From the secret book(s) about the taking away of Enoch the just, a wise man, a great scholar, whom the LORD took away, to see, to love the highest realm; and of the most wise and great, unchanging and almighty sovereignty of God, and of the very great many-eyed and immovable throne of the LORD, and of the brightly shining station of the LORD's servants, and of the ranks of the powerful, fire-born, heavenly armies, the indescribable combination of a great multitude of elements, and of the variegated appearance and indescribable singing of the army of the cherubim, and of the light without measure, to be a witness'.

The concept of 'testimony (תְּעוּדָה) occurs in the apocalyptic literature This concept is rare in the Old Testament. Beside late texts such as Sirach, it occurs – apart from Ruth 4:2 – only in Isaiah (8:16, 20) where in fact it indicates divine testimony. In the apocalyptic texts, the concept signifies a divine instruction, often concerning sacred times to be observed (because of the closeness of the Hebrew root *'wd* to the idea of establishing). Thus this concept is found repeatedly in the *Book of Jubilees*, now also attested among the Qumran documents (cf 4QJubilees = 4Q216, *DJD* XIII, II 5; IV 4; VII 17, cf the Prologue of *Jubilees* and Chapters 1-2 in Charlesworth's edition, vol I).[58]   In

---

[57] According to version A in J. H. CHARLESWORTH, *The Old Testament Pseudepigrapha* I. *Apocalyptic Literature and Testaments*, Garden City N. Y.: Doubleday 1983, p. 103-105, edited by F. I. ANDERSEN.

[58] For the Qumran texts, cf now the concordance: *The Dead Sea Scrolls concordance by* MARTIN G. ABEGG, JR., with JAMES E. BOWLEY & EDWARD M. COOK & in consultation with EMANUEL TOV, Leiden: Brill 2003.

Jubilees, the concept of 'testimony' appears beside those of 'law' and 'commandments', and so in a semantic field of revelation.

The concept of תְּעוּדָה is quite common in the texts of the first cave at Qumran, particularly in the War Scroll (1QM).[59] Its significance varies between 'established times' and 'testimonies'. Of particular importance are some texts which speak of 'testimony' in the sense of a divine destiny for men (1QH 1:19f; 1QS 3:16). Nearer to the use of the Fourth Gospel are a further two or three texts. One (1QM 11:8) speaks of the Anointed Ones of God, the 'seers of the testimonies' by means of whom God has revealed the times of the wars of his hand. In the second text (1QH 6:19), the Teacher of Righteousness speaks of those 'who are bound by my testimony'. We do well to think of the disciples of the Teacher as the recipients of this testimony (cf 1QH 2:37, 39). Thus, the text comes close to Is 8:16, 20.

One of the characteristic formulas of the fourth Gospel for the theme of testimony is 'testimony for the truth' (μαρτυρεῖν τῇ ἀληθείᾳ). This formula is found in Jn 5:33 attributed to the Baptist and in Jn 18:37 attributed to Jesus. Cf the same formula in 3 Jn 3 with an 'ecclesiastical' sense (the 'truth' becomes a synonym for the life of faith and love). For this idea of the 'testimony to the truth', recent authors refer to 1QS 8:6. In this text, which begins at 8:1, the responsibilities of the twelve men of the Council of the Community are described. Among other things, they must be 'witnesses of the truth for judgement'. In this text, 'truth' can designate either the origin of the just judgement of the members of the Council or the goal of their judgement: to cause the truth to be discovered and valued. In either case, 'truth' does not seem yet to have the significance of divine revelation as in the Fourth Gospel.

3. *The testimony about Jesus*

In two texts, the Fourth Gospel knows the use of the verb μαρτυρεῖν for the witnessing of a fact that is connected to the person, the work and the destiny of Jesus. In Jn 19:35, the word is attested with the objective accusative: 'he who saw it has given testimony' concerning what he has

---

[59] For these texts, cf J. BEUTLER, *Martyria*, 138-144.

seen, that is the opening of the side of Jesus and the outpouring of water and blood from that very side. In the second case, in Jn 21:24, someone gives testimony to what he has seen: in this case it is the evangelist bearing witness, or else the final redactor of the Gospel. The construction is different from the typically Johannine one, for μαρτυρεῖν περί τινος is used with a genitive of a thing, not of a person. We can see in these two cases developments of the Johannine vocabulary and thought, ever at the service of the Christological message of the fourth evangelist. We should not forget the testimony to Jesus given by the Samaritan Woman in Jn 4:39, expressed with μαρτυρεῖν in the absolute state: he told her all that she ever did.

Lecture XIX

The Testament

Bibliography:

J. BEUTLER, *Habt keine Angst. Die erste johanneische Abschieds-rede (Joh 14)* (SBS 116, Katholisches Bibelwerk; Stuttgart 1984), pp. 15-19; E. CORTÈS, *Los discursos de adiós de Gn 49 a Jn 13-17. Pistas para la historia de un género literario en la antigua literatura judía* (Barcelona 1976); H.-J. MICHEL, *Die Abschiedsrede des Paulus an die Kirche Apg 20,17-38. Motivgeschichte und theologische Bedeutung* (StANT 35, Kösel, Munich 1973); J. MUNCK, *«Discours d'adieu dans le Nouveau Testament et dans la littérature biblique», Aux sources de la tradition chrétienne* (FS. A. Goguel, Neuchâtel-Paris 1950), 155-170. E. STAUFFER, 'Abschiedsreden', *RAC* I (1950) 29-35; ID., *Die Theologie des Neuen Testaments* (Stuttgart ²1948); E. VON NORDHEIM, *Die Lehre der Alten* I. *Das Testament als Literaturgattung im Judentum der hellenistisch-römischen Zeit* (ALGHJ 13, Brill, Leiden 1980).

From the concept of testimony we shall now turn our attention to that of testament. Between the two concepts and their use in John, there is not only a linguistic but also a thematic similarity. The last testimony of Jesus is also his testament which is found in the Farewell Discourses of John 13-17. These discourses contain not only many themes that are common to Judaism; they also have a form which finds its antecedents and parallels in Judaism at the turn of the era. It remains true, however, that the literary genre of 'testament' is also found outside the Biblical tradition.

1. *Farewell Discourses in antiquity*

Some authors such as Stauffer[60] quote examples of farewell discourses in classical antiquity. The problem remains that the examples which he has given display few common elements between them and the texts of the New Testament.

---

[60] *Abschiedsreden* 29f.

In their commentaries on John, W. Bauer and R. Bultmann, refer to the Gnostic texts for the literary genre of farewell discourse; these too have not convinced many interpreters of the Fourth Gospel.

Thus it is more suitable to search for true parallels in the Old Testament, in the Jewish literature of the Second Temple period and in the New Testament.

2. *Farewell Discourses in the Old Testament and in the Jewish and Christian literature*

A first summary was presented by Stauffer.[61] His catalogue of parallels has been improved and fine-tuned by Munck (159-169). The New Testament parallels have been listed and studied by H.-J. Michel (35-72) and F. Cortès. Apart from Cortès, the parallels in the Old Testament and in Judaism have been studied, principally by von Nordheim.

Cortès (54) lists the following as common elements of the farewell discourses in the Intertestamental period; 'The dying person (or the person who is to be lifted up to heaven) summons his own relations, friends or followers to speak to them. 2. He delivers his exhortations. Particularly frequent among these are mention of works of mercy, love and fraternal charity, and harmony. 3. Some declarations concerning the future of the community or about the end of the ages are found at the end of the discourse'. The texts to which the author refers are almost all Intertestamental or Christian. In the canonical Old Testament, Chapters 4 and 14 of the Book of Tobit can be thought of as examples of this literary genre. The other Jewish examples are taken from the apocalyptic literature and from the *Testaments of the Twelve Patriarchs*. In the New Testament, the classic example of the farewell discourse (beside Jn 13-17) is the speech of Paul at Miletus, Acts 20:17-38.

Some other elements can be found in the farewell discourses without always being necessarily present.: 1. The person 'calls'

---

[61] *Theologie*, 327-330.

(qr'/καλεῖν) his sons or grandsons; 2. 'charges' ($ṣwh$/ἐντέλλεσθαι) his own to observe the commandments; 3. addresses them as 'sons' (τέκνα μου) particularly in connection with the foretelling of the future.[62]

According to Cortès,[63] three elements have had an influence on the genre of farewell discourse: an apocalyptic element (the foretelling of the future in a situation of tension), an element of *midrash* (the reinterpretation or actualisation of a Biblical text) and a Sapiential element (the search for a good understanding of oneself and for a just relationship with created things, with other men and with the Creator). To this element, among other things, belongs the address as 'sons'.

The similarity of the farewell addresses to the literary genre of *midrash* is of particular importance for the interpretation of Jn 13-17. It seems that the literary genre of the farewell address originated in Judaism at a time when the canon of Sacred Scripture was more or less closed. The authors who write farewell discourses use Old Testament texts as models or points of departure for the final discourse of a hero. The first examples of this technique are found in the Targum on the occasion of the Blessing of Jacob in Gen 49:1f, for example, where the text of the Targum records the words of the dying patriarch with predictions about the future together with exhortations, and also the various reactions of his sons. In its turn the apocryphal literature develops the farewell situations of the great men of Israel. Among the examples given by Cortès,[64] we could quote the expansion by *Jubilees* (20:1-20) of the narrative of Abraham's farewell in Gen 25:5, the expansion of the last words of Isaac in Gen 27:1-45; 35:27-29 in *Jub* 36:7-10; 37:4f or the expansion of the note on the assumption of Enoch in Gen 5:24, cf 22, in the apocryphal literature about Enoch, Ethiopic Enoch, for example (*1En* 93:2!) and Slavic Enoch (*2 En* XIIf). For examples taken from the literature of Hellenistic Judaism, cf Munck (158f).

---

[62] CORTÈS 56-61.
[63] *Op cit*, 62-70.
[64] Op cit, 64-66.

3. *Farewell Discourses in Jn 13-17*

Jn 14: Among the three elements listed by Cortès as essential, we find here at least the second and third. Jesus gives his last instructions to his own. The verb ἐτέλλεσθαι is not found with reference to the instructions given by Jesus but only with regard to the obedience of Jesus (14:31); however, the noun ἐντολή is found in the introductory part (13:34f) and, together with the synonym λόγος in Jn 14:15-24. the foretelling of the future is found throughout the chapter, above all in the final section, vv 25-29. The intercession, another element typical of the farewell discourses, is attested in vv 13f, 16f and 26. Throughout the chapter, the imminent departure of Jesus is presupposed, being mentioned explicitly in 13:1. Jesus will be going away (ὑπάγειν, πορεύεσθαι) and will not speak for much longer (14:30).

The technique of *midrash* is found throughout the chapter. According to the interpretation given above, vv 1-14 are inspired by Ps 42-43 and in this way by the Hebrew 'Writings'; vv 15-24 by the Deuteronomic texts; vv 25-29 by the great prophetic traditions of the Old Testament. This recourse to the great scriptural traditions of Israel is justified by the fact that beside *midrash haggadah* (that is, narrative) there also exists in Israel *midrash halakah* (that is, regulatory). To this type, vv 15-24 would correspond. The recourse to the 'Writings' and prophetic traditions remains, for its part, within the ambit of literary and theological possibilities in the period of the Second Temple.

Jn 15:1-16:4a: This 'intermediate discourse' is less characteristic of the literary genre of the farewell discourse, but it does not lack some elements of this genre. Two motifs which belong there and which can be found in our text can be highlighted: the 'commandment' and the theme of brotherly love (cf 15:9-17).

The *Testaments of the Twelve Patriarchs* are quite close to our passage. The Patriarchs 'command their sons and grandsons to observe the 'commandments' of the Lord.[65] Among the various command-

---

[65] *TLev* 13:1; 19:1; *TJud* 13:1; 29:1; *TRub* 5:1; *TDan* 5:1; 5:3 love God; *TAsher* 6:1; *TJos* 18:1; *TBenj* 3:1: "Love the Lord, observe the commandments".

ments, the commandment of love has a special role.[66] Our discussion can be broadened to examine the relationship between the New Testament in general, and John's Gospel in particular, and the Testaments of the Twelve Patriarchs.[67] According to Charlesworth, the *Testaments of the Twelve Patriarchs* were written in Greek in the middle of the second century before Christ, probably in Syria. Maccabean influence can be found in them with the emphasis on the two tribes of Judah and Levi, which correspond to the dual messianic expectation of that time and of the nascent group at Qumran. Some parallels with the New Testament which are almost literal can be explained by the hypothesis of Christian interpolations. This would be to refute the opinion of M. de Jonge according to whom the Testaments are Christian documents of the first or second centuries AD.

Jn 16:4b-33: In this section, the themes of 13:31-14:31 are taken up again. It is possible to highlight two elements that are typical of the farewell discourse. The first element is that of the hero's farewell itself. For the disciples, it will be a sadness which will later be transformed into joy (v 6, 19-22). From the point of view of Jesus, it is the promise of the Spirit-Paraclete who will continue his activity (vv 7-11; 13-15). The second element is that of the foretelling of the future. Jesus foretells not only the coming sadness, tribulation and scattering of the disciples, but also the gift of his peace and their victory alongside him. With these two elements, the text of Jn 16:4b-33 shows itself to have been influenced by the literary genre of the farewell discourse.

---

[66] *TSim* 4:7 brotherly love; cf. 7:6; *TIss* 5:2 love of God and of the neighbour with all the heart; *TRub* 5:1 mercy toward the neighbour; *TNaph* 8:2; *TJos* 19:20 unity with Levi and Judah; *TGad* 4:2 love of neighbour; 6:1 love of brother; 6:3 mutual love of the heart ; *TJos* 17:3 brotherly concord; *TBenj* 3:3 fear of the Lord and love of neighbour; 8:1, love.

[67] Cf the state of the discussion in the introduction to the English translation of the text in J. H. CHARLESWORTH, *The Old Testament Pseudepigrapha I. Apocalyptic Literature and Testaments*, Garden City N. Y.: Doubleday 1983, p. 775-783, edited by H. J. KEE, and more recently R. A. Kugler, *The Testaments of the Twelve Patriarchs* (GAP); Sheffield: SAP, 2001, especially pp 31-38, closer to de Jonge's position.

Lecture XX

The People of God

Bibliography:

S. PANCARO, '"People of God" in St John's Gospel', *NTS* 16 (1969-70) 114-129; ID., 'The Relationship of the Church to Israel in the Gospel of John', *NTS* 21 (1974-75) 396-405; J. PAINTER, 'The Church and Israel in the Gospel of John', *NTS* 25 (1978-79) 103-112; J. BEUTLER, 'Two Ways of Gathering. The Plot to Kill Jesus in John 11.47-53', *NTS* 40 (1994) 399-406; ST. MOTYER, 'The Fourth Gospel and the Salvation of Israel: An Appeal for a New Start', *Anti-Judaism and the Fourth Gospel. Papers of the Leuven Colloquium 2000*, ed. R. BIERINGER, D. POLLEFEYT, F. VANDECASTEELE-VANNEUVILLE (Jewish and Christian heritage series, 1; Assen, NL: Royal van Gorcum 2001), 92-110; F. J. MOLONEY, 'Israel, the People and the Jews in the Fourth Gospel', *Israel und seine Heilstraditionen im Johannesevangelium, Festgabe für Johannes Beutler zum 70.* Geburtstag, ed. M. LABAHN, KL. SCHOLTISSEK, A. STROTMANN (Paderborn: Schöningh 2004), 351-364.

The 'People of God' finds scant attention in the discussions about the Fourth Gospel. Almost all the related studies treat the problem of 'the Jews' in John's Gospel: a rather controversial subject (cf the next two lectures). In G. van Belle's bibliography,[68] the concepts of 'people of God' or of 'Israel' cannot be found. A few recent works are to be found by means of the bibliographical programme 'Bildi' of the University of Innsbruck (*http://bildi.uibk.ac.at*) under the key concepts 'Israel AND Johannesevangelium'.

As a framework for our discussion in this lecture, we shall take the articles of J. Painter and F. J. Moloney, at the same time bringing in the other previous works listed above.

---

[68] *Johannine Bibliography 1965-1985. A Cumulative Bibliography on the Fourth Gospel* (Collectanea Biblica et Religiosa Antiqua I), Brussel: Royal Academy 1988.

1. *The terminology*

Let us begin with some statistics: the word λαός is found in John only three times (8:2 in a text that is probably non-Johannine: the woman taken in adultery; 11:50; and 18:14); ἔθνος occurs five times (four times in Jn 11:48-52; afterwards, only in 18:35), Ἰσραήλ is found four times (1:31, 49; 3:10; 12:13); ὁ Ἰσραηλίτης once (1:47); the concept Ἰουδαῖος/Ἰουδαῖοι is much more frequent and is encountered seventy one times (Acts: 79; Synoptic together: 17; Pauline corpus: 26). It is useful to treat of the use of λαός, ἔθνος and Ἰσραήλ/Ἰσραηλίτης in their Johannine context with Painter and Moloney.

We can start from the observation that in the research of the last sixty years, right up to the nineties, the prevailing tendency was to give a clearly positive connotation to the concepts of λαός, and Ἰσραήλ/Ἰσραηλίτης in John's Gospel. This is Pancaro's position in the two articles cited above and also mine in the article of 1994 (and elsewhere). In his article, J. Painter examines this position critically. According to him, there is a development in Pancaro's position from the first article to the second. In his first contribution, Pancaro sees the λαός as open towards a new 'People of God', constituted by the Jews and Gentiles who believe in Jesus while, in his second, he seems to think of a renewed people of God made up of Jews who have arrived at faith in Jesus. In the two phases in the development of Pancaro's thought, the distinction between λαός and Ἰσραήλ/Ἰσραηλίτης as positive terms which designate the 'People of God' and ἔθνος which normally signifies 'the nations' is retained. This distinction is contested by Painter because it is attested neither in the LXX nor in the New Testament and other contemporary texts. It is necessary to return to a consideration of the point of view of the person who is speaking in the text. From the point of view of the Palestinian Jew, the citizens of the Holy Land are called Ἰσραήλ/Ἰσραηλίτης; from the point of view of foreigners, they are Ἰουδαῖοι.

A clear distinction between λαός and ἔθνος cannot be proved in John as we shall soon see. The λαός becomes 'People of God' not because of the meaning of the term itself, but from its connection with attributes such as 'People *of God*', '*his* people', '*holy* people' etc; ἔθνος can also be used for Israel if it is taken in the sense of nation and political entity (cf Jn 11:48, 50-52).

John does not lead his readers away from an old people of God to a new one; rather, from the People of God before Christ to the group of those who believe in Jesus. The People of the Old Covenant is replaced not by a new People of God but by Jesus, the 'true vine' (Jn 15:1), and by the 'flock' (ποίμνη Jn 10:16) of the Good Shepherd.

2. *The theology*

Moloney's central thesis is found in the affirmation that the concepts of Ἰσραήλ and Ἰσραηλίτης are not for John concepts that are fully positive and integrated with the Christian message. On the contrary, these concepts are expressions of a Jewish Palestinian perspective. In particular, the title 'king of Israel' does not express the Christology of the fourth evangelist, but rather the eschatological and messianic hopes of Israel in the time of Jesus. Theses expectations are, above all, political and social. A passage which confirms this view of the multiplication of the loaves according to Jn 6:1-15. Jesus has performed the great miracle of the multiplication of the loaves which has procured food for five thousand hungry people. The crowd is enthusiastic and wants to have Jesus as its king. Seeing this intention, Jesus withdraws to the mountain to pray (Jn 6:15). He does not give way to their desires. The same tension between the messianic expectations of the Palestinian Jews and the true dignity of Jesus according to John's faith community is shown in those passages that speak of Jesus or of others as 'Israelites' or of 'the king of Israel'.

A first episode is found in Jn 1:35-51. Jesus has met and called the first four disciples: a disciple who is not identified plus Andrew, Peter and Philip. Philip finds Nathaniel and tells him of his experience. Nathaniel responds sceptically: 'Can anything good come out of Nazareth?' Philip replies: 'Come and see!' So Nathaniel goes to meet Jesus. Jesus says to him: 'Behold a true Israelite, in whom is no guile' (Jn 1:47). Nathaniel remains sceptical, but when Jesus tells him that he saw him under the fig tree, Nathaniel exclaims: 'Rabbi, you are the Son of God, you are the King of Israel' (Jn 1:49). Exegetes usually take this 'profession of faith' of Nathaniel as a genuine expression of the faith of the Johannine community (cf the purpose of John in Jn 20:30f). The title of 'King of Israel' is interpreted as the title that is more clearly theological than 'Son of God'. It remains true, however, that the evangelist does not show himself fully satisfied with Nathaniel's profession of faith. So the dialogue continues: 'Jesus answered him, "Because I said to you, I saw you under the fig tree, do you believe? You shall see greater things than these." Then he adds: "Truly, truly, I say to you, you will see heaven opened, and the angels of God ascending and descending upon the Son of man"' (Jn 1:50f). Despite the clarification of the title 'King of Israel' by means of the other of 'Son of God', the evangelist does not yet feel that the richness of the Johannine faith has been exhausted. This depth is reached only with the central Christological title of 'Son of Man', the one above whom the heaven is open and on whom the angels of God ascend and descend as once they did on Jacob in his nocturnal vision (Gen 28:12; cf *supra*, Lecture XVI). It should be noted that the profession of Jesus as 'King of Israel' is found on the mouth of a Palestinian Jew in the Holy Land, not of Jesus himself or of the evangelist. Thus the approach chosen by Moloney is supported.

In Jn 3:1, Nicodemus is introduced by the evangelist as 'a ruler of the Jews'. This language corresponds to the viewpoint of the evangelist, a viewpoint taken from the Diaspora and from the Christian community. This ruler of the Jews enters into conversation with Jesus about his message and about the necessity of being born again, being born from above, of water and the Holy Spirit. Nicodemus cannot follow this sublime teaching and asks Jesus how these things can happen. So Jesus says to him: 'Are you a teacher of Israel, and yet you do not understand this?' (Jn 3:10). Once again, the name 'Israel' appears in a pre-Christian context and on the mouth of Jesus, a Palestinian Jew. We are far from the concept of the church as the 'New Israel' (cf Gal 6:16).

At this stage, it would be a good idea to recall the solemn entry of Jesus into Jerusalem according to Jn 12:12-19. The crowd coming from Jerusalem goes out to meet Jesus and hails him with the words: 'Hosanna! Blessed is he who comes in the name of the Lord, the King of Israel' (Jn 12:13). This triumphal messianic entry is not without an evangelist's comment. He connects the tradition based on the messianic-eschatological Psalm 118 (117) with the words of the prophets, in particular Zechariah, which specify the nature of Jesus' royal dignity. He is coming, not on a war horse but on a donkey. At this time, the true dignity of Jesus does not yet appear, not even to his disciples. They understand the significance of the royal entry of Jesus into the capital only after Easter, after the resurrection of the dead (Jn 12:16). The true dignity of Jesus is revealed only in the perspective of Easter, of his death and resurrection as works of salvation realised by God and acepted in faith.

In this way, Moloney's thesis that the title 'King of Israel' does not exhaust the faith of John's community but needs to be interpreted more deeply is confirmed. Jesus is 'king of Israel' only as the one who must suffer, die and rise, as the Son of Man who must be lifted up and glorified (cf Jn 12:20-36).

It remains to explain the concepts of λαός and ἔθνος in John. The chief passage for reference is in the scene of the decision of the Sanhedrin to put Jesus to death (Jn 14:47-53). A particular problem is raised from the fact that in this passage the concept of ἔθνος is employed, so it seems, for the people of Israel (Jn 11:48, 50-52), contrary to the generally accepted use of speaking of Isarel with the concept of λαός. Scholars frequently seek refuge in the thesis which states that at this moment, Israel is in process of losing its privilege of being the 'people' of God and becoming only ἔθνος, a nation like all the others. We have already seen that this argument is unsound (cf, *supra* section 1).

For this reason, therefore, it is appropriate to examine F. J. Moloney's thesis that the two concepts are largely synonymous and that the change of terminology could be caused by a change of perspective. In this passage, the concept of ἔθνος is used in a double sense: either to designate the people of Israel as a political and social unit, or to distinguish the people of the Covenant from a new people made up of the 'sons of God' gathered up by Jesus in his work of redemption. In the first sense, the concept occurs in Jn 12:48 and 12:50 (cf also 18:35). First, the members of the Sanhedrin debate the fact that, if Jesus continues with his activity, the Romans will come and take away their 'place' (the Sanctuary, or their position) and their 'people' (ἔθνος). The people is seen in this verse as a political unit which can be gained or lost. The same concept recurs in the words of Caiaphas. In the capacity of High Priest 'that year' and invested with the prophetic ability to interpret the present and the future, Caiaphas proposes that one man be sacrificed for the 'people' (λαός) instead of allowing the whole nation (ἔθνος, v 50) to perish. The 'nation' is, again, the people of Isarel regarded as a political unit. This nation must not perish, and for that it is necessary to sacrifice one person.

The concept of λαός which is found in the same verse is open to a more profound significance. According to the prophetic word of Caiaphas, Jesus has to die for the 'people', here understood as a religious entity and one open to future expansion without becoming a technical term for a the 'People of God'. This future expansion will take place only with the death and resurrection of Jesus, heralded by the arrival of the 'Greeks' to see Jesus in Jn 12:20.

In verses 51 and 52, the concept of ἔθνος is utilised twice to designate the people of Israel as opposed to other 'sons of God' who are still scattered whom Jesus will gather by means of his salvific death. It is not necessary to see in these scattered sons of God the Jews of the Diaspora as is suggested by Pancaro in his second article. Scholars usually see in these scattered sons of God all the future faithful people who will make up the flock of the Good Shepherd. As for Jn 10:16, there is similarity and difference between the concepts. In Jn 10:16, given the huge influence of Jer 23 and Ezek 34 on this chapter (cf *supra*, Lecture XIII), one could think again of the Israelites of the Diaspora. In Jn 11, on the other hand, the openness is manifest, and the perspective is directed to the whole of humanity which awaits its unity and salvation in Jesus. A confirmation of this view is found at the end of the section where (with Johannine irony) the Pharisees say: 'The whole world has gone after him' (Jn 12:19), and in the arrival of the Greeks to see Jesus (12:20).

Another buttress for this interpretation is found in the Prologue of John which Moloney cites in this respect. The Divine Word enters into the world. His own do not receive him; but there will be others who will open themselves to him. 'But to as many as received him, he gave them the power to become the sons of God, even to them who believe on his name, who were born not of blood, nor of the will of the flesh, nor of the will of man, but of God' (Jn 1:12f).

Lecture XXI

The Jews in John's Gospel (I)

Bibliography:

M. LOWE, 'Who were the Ἰουδαῖοι?', *NT* 18 (1976) 101-130; U. VON WAHLDE, 'The Johannine 'Jews': A Critical Survey,' *NTS* 28 (1928) 33-60; J. BEUTLER, 'Die 'Juden' und der Tod Jesu im Johannesevangelium,' ID., *Studien zu den johanneischen Schriften* (SBAB 25; Stuttgart: Kath. Bibelwerk 1988), 59-76; ID., 'The Identity of the 'Jews' for the Readers of John', *Anti-Judaism and the Fourth Gospel. Papers of the Leuven Colloquium*, 2000, ed. R. BIERINGER, D. POLLEFEYT, F. VANDECASTEELE-VANNEUVIVLLE (Jewish and Christian Heritage Series, 1; Assen, NL: van Gorcum 2001), 229-238; The editors of the preceding volume, 'Wrestling with Johannine Anti-Judaism: A Hermeneutical Framework for the Analysis of the Current Debate,' ibid., 3-44; A. REINHARTZ, 'The Grammar of Hate in the Gospel of John: Reading John in the Twenty-First Century,' *Israel und seine Heilstraditionen im Johannesevangelium. Festgabe für Johannes Beutler SJ zum 70. Geburtstag*, ed. M. LABAHN, K. SCHOLTISSEK, A. STROTMANN (Paderborn: Schöningh 2004), 416-427.

The subject of this lecture has already been prepared for by the previous lecture on the People of God. In its introductory section, we have already seen some statistics on the use of Johannine vocabulary in this field and on the use of Ἰουδαῖος in John.

The question of the role of the Jews in John has become ever more pressing in the last thirty years. The question could be introduced by the, apparently banal, question as to whether to write 'Jews' or Jews in John, that is, with or without inverted commas. If it is written with the commas, it signifies that these people are a specific group within Judaism whether from the social or from the historical and geographical point of view. If it is written without punctuation, then this signifies that the Jews of whom John is speaking are the Jewish people and the community of Jewish faith without any geographical, social or historical distinction. This is the opinion of A. Reinhartz in the Louvain collection.[69] Given the negative connotation of the concept in almost all the texts that are typically Johannine, there follows the impression of a Johannine anti-Jewishness? In a second article, the author, who is a Jewess, speaks even of a 'grammar of hate' in John (cf *supra*, bibliography). Is John, therefore, anti-Jewish? Does he inspire hatred against the Jews?

In these two lectures, we shall be following the introductory article by the three Belgian editors of the Louvain collection. In this contribution, the three authors present a fine summary of the volume of six hundred pages, while giving also their personal estimate.

According to the authors, five questions are discussed in the aforementioned volume:
   1) Is the Gospel of John anti-Jewish?
   2) Who are 'the Jews' in John?
   3) The separation between community and synagogue.
   4) Is there a Christology of replacement in John?
   5) The necessity of a hermeneutic of the texts.

1. *Is the Gospel of John anti-Jewish?*

We have already begun to introduce this problem. Scholars distinguish various levels on which to see a Johannine anti-Jewishness. A first level is that of John's interpreters. According to authors who see things this way, John himself is not anti-Jewish. His text is inspired by Jewish traditions and is certainly not free from polemic, but one cannot accuse the fourth evangelist of an anti-Jewish tendency. Such a tendency is to be found only in his interpreters and in the use of Johannine texts for anti-Jewish propaganda throughout the centuries (as is affirmed, among other texts, by the Holy See's 'We remember' of 1998 commemorating the *Shoah*). The Louvain editors see my contribution to their volume as also following this line of interpretation. When John speaks of the Ἰουδαῖοι, I maintain that we should think rather of a restricted group of Jewish leaders ('Jews') in Jerusalem, and

---

[69] Pp. 341-356: "'Jews' and Jews in the Fourth Gospel'.

not the whole of the people. Only because of the insertion of the Fourth Gospel in the New Testament, the term would have then acquired the general connotation of 'members of the ethnic and religious community of Israel', thus incriminating not only a Jewish group in Jerusalem but the whole people of wanting to kill Jesus.

A second group of authors sees the anti-Jewishness in this or that form in the text of the Fourth Gospel itself or else in its author. Again, it is possible to distinguish various hypotheses concerning anti-Jewishness in John and in his Gospel. Some authors seek to explain the Johannine polemic against οἱ Ἰουδαῖοι with a reference to the date of John's Gospel. In the first century AD, we encounter polemic among the various groups of Judaism (above all at Qumran) and it is an apocalyptic tendency to see one's religious opponent as representing the devil or the eschatological forces of evil. This is the opinion of J. D. G. Dunn (formerly of Durham) who, however, does not wish to exempt John from every taint of anti-Jewishness. Other scholars point to the fact that in the Judaism of the second half of the first century the Jews and Christians stand almost alone. It is not to be wondered at, therefore, if among them there is competition and polemic over the question as to which of them is the true heir of Jewish traditions. Other students, however, are more ready to accuse the author of the Fourth Gospel of anti-Jewishness. If the summary of the Christian faith is the love of God lived out by men, it is not possible to accept the 'grammar of hate' of the Fourth Gospel and its verdict on the Ἰουδαῖοι as 'sons of the devil' (Jn 8:44). This judgement is not balanced with the words of Jesus according to which 'salvation is of the Ἰουδαῖοι' (4:22).

It is fair to admit, then, that the author of the Fourth Gospel is not free of anti-Jewish sentiments. The three Louvain authors quote my observation that the word of God has its human aspect, becomes flesh and can be infected with human sin. 'We have this treasure in clay vessels' (2 Cor 4:7).

2. Who are 'the Jews' (οἱ Ἰουδαῖοι) in John?

One of the major problems of the Fourth Gospel is the use which the author makes of the concept of Ἰουδαῖοι. If we consider the fact that he himself was of Jewish origin, along with the members of the first Christian communities, why does he use this term to designate οἱ Ἰουδαῖοι who have not come to faith in Jesus? Another problem is raised by the fact that the group of people to whom he refers when he speaks of 'the Jews' seems somewhat limited: a group of people responsible for the religious life of the country with their seat in Jerusalem.

To reach a valuation of the literary data, we should observe the distinction between 'referent' and 'meaning' proposed by J. Ashton, among others, and taken up by R. Culpepper in the volume which we are looking at (cf the introduction to the Louvain volume). The referent is the person or group of people to whom the text is referring in the historical situation, the meaning is the use which the author makes of this concept in his narrative strategy.

What, then, is the referent of οἱ Ἰουδαῖοι in John's Gospel? According to an interpretation sometimes suggested,[70] the Ἰουδαῖοι of John are Christians who have recently arrived at faith in Christ and who are threatened with the danger of a new apostasy. The textual base for such a view would be Jn 8:30ff, where Jesus addresses his harshest words about the Ἰουδαῖοι as 'children of Satan' to a group of people who had (once?) 'come to faith in Jesus' (Jn 8:30f). This thesis has its value under the aspect of the use of the term in John's strategy, but it shows itself insufficient under the aspect of 'referent'. More accepted is the opinion of U. Von Wahlde and those expressed in other contributions (cf also mine), according to which the 'Jews' in John were a particular social group: the rulers of the Jewish people resident in Jerusalem. One problem for this interpretation is found in Jn 6:41 and 6:52 where such 'Jews' are located in Galilee. The problem could be solved with the hypothesis of a later origin for Jn 6, or part of this chapter, (an opinion to be taken seriously), but the majority of exegetes do not accept this theory.

Another suggestion sees the Ἰουδαῖοι in John as the residents of Judaea – whether in the broad sense as residents of the Roman province of Judaea or in the more restricted sense of residents of the southern

---

[70] H. J. DE JONGE, *et al.*

part of the country, the 'Judah' of the history of Israel (as opposed to Samaria and Galilee). This proposal has been vigorously defended by M. Lowe, but also contested, again on the ground of the two texts of Jn 6. Moreover, the term holds a connotation that is not only geographic but religious and so does not solve the problem. It should be added that the term is not reserved solely for the inhabitants of the southern region of the Holy Land, but Jesus himself appears as Ἰουδαῖος in the Fourth Gospel (4:9b, 22; 18:35).

Some authors (such as A. Reinhartz and A. R. Culpepper) highlight the problem of John's use of this term to indicate all the Jews whether of the time of Jesus or his own time (and of all time) with a term originally oriented towards a determined group within Judaism. In this choice there is a very dangerous dynamism which could favour anti-Jewishness and even more favour the anti-Semitism of our days.

If the 'referent' of the term Ἰουδαῖοι still remains uncertain, its 'meaning' appears clearer. Οἱ Ἰουδαῖοι represent all those persons who are opposed to faith in Jesus. This is how it was seen by Bultmann, and he is followed by S. Schoon and J. Zumstein. For A. Reinhartz, οἱ Ἰουδαῖοι and Jesus are the two poles of the Johannine narrative: it is betwen them that the reader has to decide. There is no choice in between.

The fact that the term οἱ Ἰουδαῖοι has a literary aim could excuse, at least in part, the author of the Fourth Gospel from the accusation of being anti-Jewish. If these Ἰουδαῖοι are only the literary expression of a narrative strategy, they do not merit the accusation of anti-Jewishness in the strict sense. However, it is emphasised by A. Reinharz that even this use is potentially anti-Jewish. If οἱ Ἰουδαῖοι are the prototype of unbelief, this accusation can easily be directed at all Jews of all times, and the consequences are clearly foreseeable.

3. *The separation between community and synagogue*

The hostility between Jesus and οἱ Ἰουδαῖοι in John finds its explanation in a conflict between the nascent Christian (Johannine) community and the synagogue. There is a general scholarly consensus that there was a conflict between these two entities. Only H. J. De

Jonge thinks that this conflict was simply a narrative tool of the evangelist to prepare his readers for a courageous decision of faith in Christ. Differences remain, however, over the time when the conflict happened and the importance of the schism for the relationship between Church and Synagogue in general in the first century. The majority of scholars think that the conflict in John's Gospel was of a local rather than a universal nature. Only Culpepper maintains that this clash had an important part to play for the future relationship between Church and Synagogue.

Who, then, were the conflicting parties? Three theories have been propounded. According to the first, the conflict was between Christians and Christians. The point of departure for this theory is the passage Jn 8:30-59, precisely that section in which οἱ Ἰουδαῖοι are called 'sons of the devil' (8:44). Jesus thus is speaking to people who have taken on board faith in him but have not come to full acceptance of the dogma of the Johannine community.[71] The Louvain editors remain sceptical towards such a suggestion. According to them, the significance of the perfect participle πεπιστευκότες is not clear: the word could signify 'who had come to faith in Jesus' or 'who had once believed in Jesus' in a pluperfect sense, something that had happened but was no longer a present reality.

According to another theory, the conflict would be between Jews and Jews. Authors like J. D. G. Dunn who promote an historical-critical reading of John tend towards a solution of this kind. Towards the middle of the first century, there was not yet a clear and neat distinction between the Jewish community and the Christian community; Christianity still appeared as a Jewish sect. Authors like Dunn and B. Klappert also emphasise the violence of the intra-Jewish debates of the period, at Qumran among others – where in the Community Rule we find an exhortation to hate the (Jewish) enemy – and in the *Testaments of the Twelve Patriarchs*. According to another author (M. C. de Boer), the term Ἰουδαῖοι in John would have been used in an ironic way to designate the false representatives of the Jewish religion. None of these

---

[71] Cf. H. J. de Jonge, H. Hoet in the Louvain volume.

proposals has convinced the editors greatly. At the centre of the debate stands the controversy over who Christ is, and this controversy goes beyond the possible themes of intra-Jewish debate.

There remains, therefore, the third possibility, one favoured also by the majority of the authors of the volume we are discussing: that the conflict took place between Johannine Christians and Jews. The argument has already been given by R. A. Culpepper among others. A linguistic argument highlighted by another author (P. Thomson) leads us to add this: οἱ Ἰουδαῖοι is an expression which is normally used to indicate Jews by non-Jews. Thus a separation which is already strongly advanced is reflected in this designation. At the centre of the debate stands the question as to whether a Jew believes in Jesus and orients his whole existence towards him or not.[72] We shall return to this point in the next lecture.

---

[72] Cf. J. Zumstein and again A. Reinhartz.

Lecture XXII

The Jews in John's Gospel (II)

Before going on with the article of R. Bieringer and others on anti-Jewishness in John, it would be best to make a little excursus on the verse which has caused so much uncertainty among exegetes: 'As he spoke thus, many believed on him'(8:30). At first sight, this verse seems isolated, and some scholars propose that it should not receive too much emphasis. Someone has even suggested that 8:31 be read: 'Jesus then spoke to those who had once believed in him'. What, then, is the significance of this faith of 'many' (Jews) in Jesus?

We shall see that this theme pervades the whole of the first part of John's Gospel; 8:30 is not an isolated case. Already in the second chapter, after the Cleansing of the Temple and the identification of Jesus with the Jewish Temple, it is noted: 'Now when he was in Jerusalem at the Passover feast, many believed in his name when they saw the signs which he did; but Jesus did not trust himself to them, because he knew all men and needed no one to bear witness of man; for he himself knew what was in man' (2:23-25). So we find among numerous Jews an initial faith which still needed to be deepened and did not yet merit the trust of Jesus (play of words with a double πιστεύειν).

The following texts are all to be found in chapters 7-12, in the section of the 'great controversies'. Already in 7:31, after a failed attempt to arrest Jesus for blasphemy, we read: 'Yet many of the people believed in him; they said, "When the Christ appears, will he do more signs than this man has done?"' The next text is that is that of Jn 8:30f. At the end of the long narrative section on the healing of the man born blind, followed by the Good Shepherd Discourse, it is reported in 10:19-21: 'There was again a division among the Jews because of these words. Many of them said, "He has a demon, and he is mad; why listen to him?" Others said, "These are not the sayings of one who has a demon. Can a demon open the eyes of the blind?"'

We could also mention the faith of many in Jesus according to Jn 10:42. However, this faith is ascribed to the inhabitants of Peraea.

More relevant is an observation made at the end of the long account of the raising of Lazarus in Jn 11:1-44. 'Many of the Jews therefore, who had come with Mary and had seen what he did, believed in him; but some of them went to the Pharisees and told them what Jesus had done' (11:45f). As in the preceding texts, John reports the two ways in which the witnesses of the works and words of Jesus react to him: with acceptance or rejection.

A last text of this kind is found in Jn 12:11. Again, the raising of Lazarus leads the Jewish authorities to take measures, in this case not only against Jesus but also against Lazarus. 'So the chief priests planned to put Lazarus also to death, because on account of him many of the Jews were going away and believing in Jesus'.

On the basis of these texts (to which it would be possible to add others such as Jn 12:19), it cannot be said that Jn 8:30 stands as an isolated case and that Jesus speaks only to the Jews who had once believed in him. Jewish believers in Jesus recur regularly in the first part of John's Gospel. What, then, is the literary function of these Ἰουδαῖοι?

The answer lies in the fact that John almost always recounts the positive reaction to Jesus together with the other reactions, critical and hostile. To the Jews who believe in Jesus correspond others who do not; on the contrary, they remain hostile and seek to kill Jesus (cf 11:47-53!).

From this, one can infer that the taking of positions towards Jesus, in the first part of John's Gospel, pursues the aim of leading the readers of John towards a clear and courageous decision of faith in Christ. Some examples of Ἰουδαῖοι who have arrived at faith in Jesus show how the evangelist wants to guide his readers too towards a prompt profession of faith in Jesus. Such examples of faith attained and professed are Nicodemus (cf his development towards a clear position in favour of Jesus from Jn 3:1-11 through 7:50f to 19:38-41), the

Samaritan Woman (Jn 4), the Man Born Blind (Jn 9) and Thomas as spokesman for the disciples (Jn 11:16). These examples are intended to convince those who have arrived at faith in Jesus to have the courage to profess it openly (cf the Jews, even Jewish leaders, who believed in Jesus but did not have the courage to profess their faith in Jn 12:42f).

Thus the fourth evangelist leads his readers to faith in Jesus: a faith inspired by the words of Jesus and not only his marvellous works, and professed even in adverse circumstances. Against this background we have also to see the passages of John's Gospel which speak of the Ἰουδαῖοι in a very negative way. For John, it is necessary to decide for Jesus without any middle course. He who does not accept the word of Jesus is no longer a son of Abraham but a son of the devil.[73]

4. *A Christology of supersession in John?*

At this point, we shall take up again the article by R. Bieringer *et al.* In section 3 of the previous lecture – 'The separation between the community and the synagogue' – we arrived at the conclusion that the conflict between οἱ Ἰουδαῖοι and the adherents of the Christian group was focused on faith in Jesus. The question, still to be clarified, is whether faith in Jesus is possible within Israel and whether all the Jewish religious institutions are still guaranteed when a Jew decides to believe in Jesus and to enter the Christian community.

Scholars vary in their reply to this question. For one group, faith in Jesus is only the fulfilment of the hopes of Israel and its institutions of salvation. This is the opinion of G. van Belle and F.-W. Marquardt. Together with B. Klappert, these authors see in Jn 4:22 the centre and peak of the Johannine theology of salvation: 'Salvation is of the Jews'. Klappert sees John's Christology as closely united with that of the Synoptics: the profession of Jesus as Messiah of Israel and Son of Man, foretold by Daniel, destined to gather and save the People of God in the

---

[73] On John's purpose, cf. J. BEUTLER, 'Faith and Confession: The Purpose of John', *Word, Theology, and Community in John*, ed. J. PAINTER - R. A. CULPEPPER - F. F. SEGOVIA, St. Louis, Chalice Press 2001, 19-31.

eschatological age. According to S. Motyer, the motif of the replacement of the Temple – the destruction of which had taken place – by the Jewish community is found also in R. Johanan b. Zakai; in this way, the replacement of the Temple with the body of Jesus according to Jn 2:21 is not far from the *Jewish* idea of supersession. Thus, according to J. Zumstein, it makes sense to speak of the 'fulfilment' rather than the replacement of the religious institutions on the part of Jesus and the Christian community. It is his opinion that Jesus is at the same time the fulfilment and the culmination of the history of Israel and the divine revelation begun in Israel.

It is the mind of the Louvain editors that one must distinguish between 'fulfilment' and 'supersession'. Fulfilment easily becomes supersession whether because of the lack of respect for the text of John on the part of exegetes or whether because of the difficulty of the text itself. Not infrequently, scholars ready to preserve Israel's way of salvation, quote Jn 4:22 but leave out Jn 8:44!

According to R. A. Culpepper, it is this same Gospel of John that leaves little room for the Jewish faith and institutions after the decision of faith in Jesus. Scholars quote Culpepper *verbatim*: 'On the one hand, the Johannine retention of so many meaningful Jewish features is the highest compliment that the daughter faith could pay to the parent faith. On the other hand, apart from all that is fulfilled in Jesus very little is left in Judaism. The gospel of John, therefore, does not dispassionately set forth the truth of the Christian faith. It claims the fulfilment of Judaism and in the process it strips Judaism of the validity of its faith and practice.' (32). According to Culpepper, Christianity continues Jewish exclusivity, transforming it into a Christian exclusivity. Outside Jesus and faith in him there is no salvation. Adele Reinhartz is of the same opinion: 'The Christology of the Fourth Gospel does not envisage salvation for non-believers such as the Jews' (*ibid*).

Apparently, Culpepper still makes a distinction between the model of supersession favoured by the fourth evangelist and a Christian exclusivity. This distinction is not accepted by A. Reinhartz according to whom a Johannine exclusivity is at the same time a Christian exclusivity. The supersession of Israel by Jesus and the Church in a canonical writing of the New Testament poses a fundamental problem for relations between Christians and Jews. Thus two possibilities remain to resolve this problem: either free John from the accusation of using the model of supersession or find new hermeneutical avenues to interpret the text of the Gospel.

5. *The necessity of a hermeneutic of the texts*

The strategy adopted by some authors is that of distinguishing between diverse literary strata and so to free the fourth evangelist from the accusation of being anti-Jewish. Thus, for J. Charlesworth, verse 14:6b, according to which no one can come to the Father except by Jesus, is an interpolation which does not do justice to the thought of the fourth evangelist. Few exegetes share this opinion. Another way out consists in attributing the references to 'the Jews' in John only to a specific group within Judaism: the Jewish rulers in Jerusalem. In my opinion, this is a possibility, but it does not work once John is seen as part of the canon. However, the text of the Fourth Gospel, at least in so far as it is included in the New Testament, cannot be exonerated from the charge of utilising a language that is anti-Jewish.

Other scholars seek a solution to the problem of the Christology of supersession by making reference to the hermeneutical rule according to which the texts must be read according to a fundamental understanding of the document to which they belong. If the heart and the centre of the New Testament is the message of love, it is impossible to consent to accepting a 'grammar of hate'. From this starting point, some scholars seek to 'deconstruct' the problematic passages of the Fourth Gospel. Thus, to 'balance' Jn 8:44, they draw attention to Jn 4:22. Here too, however, there lurks the danger of minimising the problem. Moreover, every so often, a precise interpretation of Jn 4:22 seems to be unsuccessful. We need to ask ourselves whether the sense of Jn 4:22 consists in respect for Judaism or rather in the preparation of the Samaritan Woman for a new form of faith which surpasses the institutions both of Israel and of the Samaritans.

The root problem is that of deciding if one can accept the presence of an anti-Jewish approach in John's Gospel without abandoning the authority of Scripture. The problem becomes still more serious when one considers the historical connections between anti-Jewishness and anti-Semitism.

In order to reply to the questions about the anti-Jewishness of John, the Louvain editors call for a reflection on revelation, its purpose and its limits. At this point, the authors once again cite yours truly, expressing the conviction that Sacred Scripture is at the same time Word of God and human word. As Word of God it is holy and infallible, as human word it is subject to 'incarnation', to temptation and even to sin. 'We have this treasure in clay vessels'. Other authors such as J. D. G. Dunn and R. Burggraeve are of the same opinion.

In conclusion, the editors discern three results in the recent studies: (a) the Fourth Gospel contains anti-Jewish elements; (b) the anti-Jewish elements are unacceptable from the Christian point of view; (c) it is impossible to eliminate these anti-Jewish elements from the text of the Fourth Gospel, thus conserving a kernel without any anti-Judaism. It remains necessary, therefore, to interpret John's text honestly and responsibly. At this point, the editors invite the readers to a reflection on divine revelation. If divine revelation is considered as the divine message to human beings by means of a sacred text, the problem will not go away. On the other hand, if it starts from a more dynamic understanding of revelation as a two way communication between God and man, then a new hermeneutical horizon is opened.

According to our authors, revelation is not simply identical with the sacred text. The sacred text is, on the other hand, the bearer of a divine message in human form. Divine word and human word at one and the same time, divine revelation shares also in the human limitations of the authors and enters into a world of error and sin.

The Johannine anti-Jewishness belongs to these human limitations of the Divine Word. In this sense, we can interpret the words of John's Prologue: 'And the Word was made flesh and dwelt among us...' (Jn 1:14).

Lecture XXIII

Horizons for a Jewish-Christian Dialogue on John's Gospel

Bibliography:

C. M. MARTINI, *Verso Gerusalemme* (Milan: Feltrinelli 2002), cap. III 'Le relazioni ebraico-cristiane', pp. 104-112 'Le vie del dialogo'; J. BEUTLER, 'Il Popolo Ebraico e le sue Sacre Scritture. Un nuovo documento della Pontificia Commissione Biblica', *CivCatt 153*, 1 June 2002, 444-457; ID., 'Ietro e il dialogo: proposte per il presente e per il futuro', *Verità, libertà, violenza. Un colloquio fra Ebrei e Cristiani. Atti del XXIV Colloquio ebraico-cristiano di Camaldoli* (4 – 8 dic. 2003), ed. I. GARGANO (Koinonia 13), Villa Verucchio, RN: Pazzini Publications, 2004, 33-43.

At the end of this course it would be well to draw some conclusions from the subjects and texts that we have studied. I would like to highlight here aspects of a future Jewish-Christian dialogue that takes John's Gospel as its basis.

1. *An honest dialogue*

Every Jewish–Christian dialogue on John's Gospel must have an awareness of the problematic role of the Jews in the Fourth Gospel. This problem was set out in all its seriousness in the last lecture. By contrast with the approach at the time of the nineteen seventies, when it was still possible to excuse the language of the Fourth Gospel by limiting its expression to a restricted social group within Judaism (the residents of Judaea, the Jewish rulers in Jerusalem etc), today the tragic dimension of the choice of the expression οἱ Ἰουδαῖοι to designate the enemies of Jesus in John is recognised. Adele Reinharz has insisted on the gravity of the expression, emphasising that οἱ Ἰουδαῖοι signifies the Jews without inverted commas with all the consequences that derives from such a practice: the Jews are opposed to Jesus, they seek to arrest him and to stone him, and in they end they hand him over to the Roman authorities for execution. They are 'sons of the devil' and no longer sons of Abraham.

A dialogue between Jews and Christians must always take account of these facts and of their consequences in the course of history: from the exclusion of the Jews from the *societas christiana* during the Middle Ages and the Modern Era to their imprisonment in the ghettos from the sixteenth century onwards; from the *pogroms* over many centuries to the *Shoah*.

In Rome, there is no lack of witnesses to the situation of the Jews in the Papal city in medieval and modern times. Let us look at one of them. Near to the double bridge over the Tiber at Isola Tiberina, on the left bank of the river, you will find the Church of S. Gregorio della Divina Pietà, in the immediate neighbourhood of the former Jewish ghetto. Above the doorway of the church, we can still read today an inscription in Hebrew which at first sight could even seem to be an expression of the common faith of Jews and Christians in the city. In this case, however, it attests to the contrary. The text of the inscription is taken from the Book of Isaiah: 'All the day long, I held out my hands to a disobedient and gainsaying people' (Is 65:2). Several centuries ago, on this spot, which was part of the Papal States, a curious ceremony used to take place: the Jewish community of the ghetto had to assemble before this church every Good Friday to listen to a sermon of condemnation and penitence. This was a condition of their enjoying the privilege of living in the Holy City for a further year. At that time it was also customary every year to pray in the Good Friday Liturgy 'for the perfidious Jews', an intercession which was replaced only by Pius XII in 1951.

Not far from S. Gregorio della Divina Pietà, on the other bank of the Tiber, you come across the Rabbinic Seminary with a commemorative tablet which records the deportation of the Jews from the city during the occupation by the Nazis. For the Jews, there is a certain continuity between the one persecution and the other.

2. *An open dialogue*

Another element of the dialogue between Jews and Christians must be the readiness to listen and to learn. If one of the two parties is convinced that it is in exclusive possession of the truth, the dialogue does not exist except to confirm the other party in its own convictions. A true and authentic Jewish-Christian dialogue must start from the conviction that each can learn something from the other.

In 2001, the Pontifical Biblical Commission published a document in which the principles of such a dialogue, based on the common Bible of Jews and Christians, are developed. For the Christian who reads the Sacred Scripture of Israel with the eyes of faith in Jesus as Messiah of Israel and Son of God, a problem presents itself from the fact that, if the Jews reads the same Bible without such faith, then he is in error. This has been the conviction of Christians for many centuries. One thinks of the image of the Synagogue, with its eyes blindfolded, over the side door of Strasbourg Cathedral. The image of the Church over the same door is able to see; the Synagogue on the other hand cannot. It is blind.

The Biblical Commission has sought to suggest another way of looking at things. In the sections which begin and conclude the chapter on the 'Fundamental common themes of the Jewish and Christian Bibles', the authors propose to see in the sense which the Christian reader discovers in the Scripture of Israel an added dimension which surpasses that originally discovered by the Jewish reader. I quote from the document of the Pontifical Biblical Commission (n 21): 'Although the Christian reader is aware that the internal dynamism of the Old Testament finds its goal in Jesus, this is a retrospective perception whose point of departure is not in the text as such, but in the events of the New Testament proclaimed by the apostolic preaching. It cannot be said, therefore, that Jews do not see what has been proclaimed in the text, but that the Christian, in the light of Christ and in the Spirit, discovers in the text an additional meaning that was hidden there.' With the expression 'an additional meaning', the document takes up a concept of modern semantics that has been developed, for example, by Paul Ricoeur. According to that concept, texts do not simply contain an objective sense which remains immutable for readers of every time and place. On the contrary, all texts from the past possess a 'history of their reception', something also underlined by H.-G. Gadamer. In the final analysis, texts do not simply 'have' a sense but acquire it continually by means of every one of their interpreters. Each interpreter does not create a new sense but discovers it each time in a new way through which he is also able to bring to light dimensions of the text which up to that moment have remained hidden to its interpreters. At the end of the second part, the document returns once more to this concept (n 64): 'Christian readers were convinced that their Old Testament hermeneutic, although significantly different from that of Judaism, corresponds nevertheless to a potentiality of meaning that is really present in the text. Like a "revelation" during the process of photographic development, the person of Jesus and the events concerning him now appear in the Scriptures with a fullness of meaning that could not be hitherto perceived. Such a fullness of meaning establishes a threefold connection between the New Testament and the Old: continuity, discontinuity, and progression.' In this perspective, an opening is provided for the Jewish reader towards the Christian reading as a possible interpretation of the sacred texts of Israel. On the other hand, the Christian must remain open to the richness of Jewish interpretation in general and of Rabbinic exegesis in particular. This is underlined by the document in the first chapter (n 22).

3. *A constructive dialogue*

In his contribution, Cardinal Martini has suggested some stages of a common way for Christians and Jews. For the Christian, prayer finds its most concentrated expression in the celebration of the Eucharist. In this the Christian meets with the Jew for whom the *Berakhà* and the *Todah* accompany the whole day and all of life.

Conversion or *teshuvah* is the second step required. This is necessary for both the individual and the community whether in Christianity or Judaism. Together with prayer directed to God for the pardon of our sins, as Christians, we should try to seek pardon for the sins committed against the Jews and try to banish all prejudices from our thought. 'Let us return to God, and to the man who is his image; let us bend down to our Jewish brother, to the history of his sufferings, his martyrdom, the persecutions he has undergone' (107).

In third place, C. M. Martini suggests study and dialogue, *Talmud Torah*. On the Christian side, this means interest in the particular scientific, juridical, philosophical and theological tradition of Judaism which has been developed in the centres of study dedicated to it. It is thus that initiatives to discover the rich Talmudic tradition of the Jewish religion can be encouraged. In part, Christian prejudices against Judaism are caused by ignorance of this tradition.

The fourth step is to be the universal dialogue which brings in other interlocutors to share the dialogue beside Jews and Christians. The dialogue with the Islamic religion would be of particular interest, and that for two reasons: the closeness of Islam to Judaism and Christianity because of its monotheism and its roots in the Abrahamic tradition, and the geographical closeness of the two monotheistic religions in the Holy Land and Jerusalem. The Cardinal adds: 'Judaism offers many examples of openness to dialogue not only with Islam but also with other religions and with science and philosophy. *A propos* of this dialogue, we can recall, among Christians, the recent examples of Louis Massignon and Charles de Foucald; let us also recall Giorgio La Pira whom I was able to meet often on the occasion of Jewish-Christian conferences in the interest of the East' (109).

A fifth step is added: that of initiatives. 'The approach to the Jewish piety and culture can be cultivated at various levels. At the level of study, promoting meetings and research, and coordinating what already exists; in the schools, using possibilities provided by the educational laws and revising textbooks; it would then be possible to arrange courses of renewal for the clergy and catechists and to set up courses and initiatives in seminaries and in dioceses' (*ibid*).

In December 2003, I was able to share in the XXIVth Jewish-Christian Colloquium of Camaldoli with the paper published in the Acts under the title 'Jethro and Dialogue: proposals for the present and the future'. The organisers had chosen the figure of Jethro as the theme because Moses' father in law offers some aspects that are relevant to the inter-religious dialogue. He was a Midinaite priest, and so the representative of another people and another religion. This fact did not prevent Moses from accepting him as father in law, marrying his daughter and having two sons by her in the land of Midian (cf Ex 2:16-22; 3:1f; 4:18;18). In one particular case, Moses who was the sole judge of the people and overburdened with responsibilities, accepted the advice of his father in law and instituted fellow judges, committing to them the judgment of easy cases while reserving to himself the more serious and difficult ones. The putting into practice of this advice lightened the burden of administering justice for Moses (Ex 18).

In the paper cited above, I drew some conclusions from the example of Moses, Jethro's son in law. A first conclusion: 'To overcome prejudice and arrive at friendship with 'the other', it is necessary to go to him. Moses would not have made friends with Jethro and his daughter if he had not left Egypt and gone to the Land of the Midianites' (39).

The second: 'Beyond going to the place where the other lives, it is necessary also to listen to the other and take his advice' (40). One could highlight at this point the importance of the collaboration of the adherents of various religions and confessions in the social field, for example in the work for refugees.

'An important element in the Biblical texts examined was the marriage with women of another people and another religion' (*ibid*). I also made reference to the example of the marriage between Boaz and Ruth, the Moabitess, ancestress of King David. Often, 'mixed' marriages are seen as wrong in the various religions. More recently there has been seen also the possibility that such marriages may contribute to the coming near of two religions.

A final element which the case of Moses and Jethro teaches us is that of the common meal, as it is recorded in Ex 18:12. The experience teaches us that such common meals – the problem of *kasherut* (rules concerning foods legal and forbidden to Jews) having been overcome – can contribute notably to the friendship and mutual knowledge of Jews and Christians as also of the representatives of other religions. In the great cities of the Western world, local fiestas and street parties, even community feasts open to all give the lived example of such fraternity. In this context, the text of Exodus also mentions a common sacrifice of Moses and his people with Jethro and his family. Exegetes of the past have asked themselves the question as to what kind of sacrifice is in question here and to what divinity Moses and Jethro would have offered such a common sacrifice. According to St Thomas, for example, it was unimaginable that Jethro would have remained 'pagan' after so many years of living with Moses. However, this kind of argument goes beyond the text. The text itself invites us to welcome occasions of common religious service for the adherents of various religions, above all in services of prayer for peace. Pope John Paul II himself gave us the example in his prayer with the members of other religions at Assisi in October 1986. The example was followed in another city also, Frankfurt. Perhaps it would be too much to ask the adherents of other religions to pray directly together with Christians and Jews. If, however, each addresses the Creator in his own language of prayer, this is a precious sign of the peace which is being desired and a pledge of that peace itself.

INDEX OF AUTHORS

166

CONTENTS

Stampa: Dicembre 2006

presso la tipografia
"Giovanni Olivieri" di E. Montefoschi
Roma • info@tipografiaolivieri.it